KINGDOM OF JOY

TALES FROM RUMI

Abdul Rahman Azzam

Illustrations
by
Fatima Zahra Hassan

Produced by
Bookchase UK Ltd.

Design by
Khalida Rahman

ISBN 0-946079-89-7

Note:

After the Prophet's name, there appears the Arabic letter *sad*, (ﷺ), standing for: *Salla'Llahu'alayhi wa alihi wa sallam* [God bless him and his Family, and give them peace]. After the names of the Imams and of the Prophet's daughter, Fatima, there appears the Arabic letter *ayn*, (ع) standing for: *'Alayhi (or 'alayha* or *alayhim) al-Salam* [Peace be with him (or her or them)].

Contents

Preface

The name of Mawlana Jalal ud-Din Rumi is becoming increasingly popular in the West. In the centuries after his death in 1273 his fame spread through the countries of the Muslim East, from Konya, where the green dome of his Mausoleum shines in radiant beauty, to Bengal. From the late 18th century, parts of his work were rendered into European languages, and a daily increasing number of books and articles on his work are being published. We find versions of his Mathnavi, the great Persian poem that was called by Jami 'the Qur'an in Pahlavi', comprising more than 25,000 couplets in Turkish, Urdu, Sindhi, Bengali, and moreover into English, Czech, French, German, Swedish and Italian. For Rumi's wisdom is not restricted to the people of one nation; it is universal.

However, the 'Spiritual Couplets' have been illuminated only rarely, for example in some Persian prints of the 19th century. This was because the feeling that a religious book should not be filled with pictures of living beings prevailed, as it indeed still does in most of the Islamic countries. However, a young Pakistani artist has been inspired by the stories, which are taken from both the Mathnavi and Rumi's work *Fihi ma Fihi*, written in prose. Coming from a country where miniature painting was an important part of art, she has taken up some topics in a style that originates in her

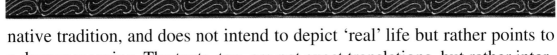

native tradition, and does not intend to depict 'real' life but rather points to a deeper meaning. The texts, too, are not exact translations, but rather interwoven with the translator's commentaries which make it easier to understand the deeper meaning of Rumi's simple stories.

Thanks to the cooperation of a scholar who retells the most famous of Rumi's stories, and a young lady painter from the Indo-Pakistani tradition of miniature painting, Rumi's thought can be enjoyed by everyone, readers of different ages and backgrounds, and I hope that it will form a useful introduction to the work of the most eloquent and most lovable, the wisest and the most humane writer in the Islamic Sufi tradition.

Professor Annemarie Schimmel
Bonn, Germany
2002

Acknowledgements

When I was asked to write 'Tales of Rumi', the publisher stipulated that the work should be done within a year. He could so easily have stipulated a lifetime, such is the breadth and diversity of Rumi's Mathnavi.

'I have not sung the Mathnavi,' Rumi wrote, 'for you to hold it or repeat it, but to put it under your feet, so you could fly. The Mathnavi is the ladder toward the truth.' The Mathnavi is a book filled with stories and parables, legends and fables. Rumi starts a story, drops it, and then takes it up again; a story grows out of a tale that transforms itself into a mystical teaching. Occasionally, a word or even a sound begins a story. The overall effect is dazzling and brilliant, if somewhat confusing. And yet underlying these seemingly random stories about mice, parrots, peacocks and frogs, is Rumi's profound understanding and love for the Qur'an.

Every story in the Mathnavi is a parable, transmitting a moral and mystical truth. The stories, some humorous, others sad, are all striking, and if the details are forgotten, once recalled they carry within them the mystical truths interwoven in a symbolic language that speaks to everyone according to their capacity. In one of his most amusing stories, for example, a chickpea tries to jump out of the pot in which it was being cooked. 'The water is too hot!' It yelled, 'Let me out.' But the cook would have nothing of it, and pushes the chickpea back into the cooking pot, explaining that it has to endure this trial for a while. Having grown up in God's sunshine, it now has to be able to fulfil the purpose for which it was created.

But perhaps the most famous story to be found in the Mathnavi is the one with which the poem begins. In the '*Song of the Reed*', the flute, cut from its reed bed, cries out in its longing for home, and in doing so it reveals the secret of eternal love. The key word is love. For Rumi, love is the source of the universe. It is because of love that the soul aspires to the meeting that will show it that the Lover and the Beloved are one.

An elephant saw in his dream the vast desert of your Hindustan! Hindustan stands for the eternal home that the soul recalls in a dream, and the elephant that dreams of Hindustan is like the nightingale who longs for the rose garden or the reed that pines for its reed-bed.

I would like to thank Professor Anne-Marie Schimmel, whose love for and writings on Rumi have inspired so many over the years, for an eloquent preface. I would also like to thank Fatima Zahra Hasan whose charming illustrations cannot fail to capture the beauty of Rumi's stories. A special mention also for Dr Reza Shah-Kazemi whose editing and comments were of enormous help; thanks are due also to Trevor Banyard for proof-reading, and to Khalida Rahman who not only worked so diligently on the book design, with its charming borders and chapter headings, but who was responsible, more than anyone else, for ensuring that this book came to fruition.

The moment I heard my first story
I began looking for you

Our story begins with an animal, but not just any animal. The name Balkh may provide a few clues, but its classical name, Bactria, is linked to that remarkable two-humped creature, the Bactrian camel. Not with two humps like the Arabian camel, but one; and hair, lots of hair. Indeed, one could easily imagine that the Arabian camel with its elegant, urbane stride and its proud, aloof gaze would certainly not be amused to learn that he has a hairier, more robust cousin — after all, was it not an Arabian one that carried the Prophet Muhammad (ﷺ) on his hegira to Medina? Not that it would bother the Bactrian too much, for he knows that his Arabian cousin could not survive a single winter's day in Bactria. There the temperature

can drop to as low as — 22 degrees Fahrenheit, and the camel is thankful for the long hair that is thickest around its humps, forelegs, head and neck. With the onset of summer, when temperatures may reach 122 degrees, the coat is shed to reveal a black skin that resists sunburn. Not surprisingly, given such harsh extremes in weather, the Bactrian camel needs to be strong. The camel also needs to be tough; in summer it can lose up to 40% of its body weight in water and still survive. In the winter it can go up to a week without food or drink and not die. It certainly needs that second hump, not to store water, but to store fat which it uses for energy. Unlike its Arabian cousin, the Bactrian camel may not have carried a Prophet, but it is certainly a tough animal. And if we begin our story in Balkh with the Bactrian camel, it is because it was in that city that the hero of our story, Jalal ud-Din Rumi, was born, and, such was the love that Rumi had for animals and the love that the birds and the beasts had for him, that we begin where we begin.

The Perfumer & the Parrot

There once lived in the fabled city of Baghdad a perfumer who owned a parrot. The parrot was unlike any other; he was green in plumage with eyes that sparkled with intelligence. He was also an excellent talker, and perched outside the perfumer's shop on a bench, the parrot spent his days mimicking words uttered by passers-by or commenting on what he saw.

One day, as the perfumer was away on business, the parrot, distracted by a noise, suddenly flew off. As he did so he carelessly (for parrots are notoriously careless) knocked over a bottle of rose oil, which spilled onto the bench. A little while later the owner returned to the shop and, as was his wont, sat on the bench outside of his shop as owners of shops tend to do. No sooner had he done so, however, than he noticed that his clothes had become covered in oil, and on spotting the broken bottle of rose-oil, he understood

what had taken place.

'That rascal,' he muttered to himself angrily, 'I'll teach that parrot to take more care.'
No sooner had he spoken than the parrot reappeared from wherever it had been doing what parrots do, and merrily took his place next to the owner on the bench.

'Hello!' he shrieked, for the parrot was both articulate and polite.

But the perfumer was in no mood to greet careless parrots no matter how polite, and he struck the bird on the head.

'That will teach you to spill my oils!'

Such was the shock to the poor parrot, that no sooner had the blow landed on his head than his feathers began to fall off. First in ones, then in twos, until the bird was totally bald. And if that was not enough, he went totally silent and not a single word passed his beak.

For a day or two the perfumer paid no attention, for it was not uncommon for parrots to lose their plumes. And as for not talking, well, he himself often went for days without talking. Why should a bird be unlike a man?

But if not on the third day, then certainly by the fourth, the perfumer began to worry, for though he may have struck the parrot, in reality he loved him dearly.

By the fifth day the man had become alarmed, and he now began to encourage his parrot to talk. He offered him his favourite food, he sang to him his favourite songs, he even juggled, he turned cartwheels. But all to no avail, for the parrot remained silent, simply gazing at his owner with no expression. And he remained bald.

By the second week the perfumer was in a terrible state, and he now offered good money to anyone who could make his parrot talk (or even just grow feathers). Now, money has a way of attracting people, and it was not long before a queue of supposed bird doctors was forming near the bench outside the perfumer's shop on which the parrot sat glumly. And for the next few days the most bizarre medical experiments were carried out on the sulking, silent, bald bird. The parrot was, in turn, immersed in water, rubbed in oil, danced around, hypnotised, chanted to, doused in powder, made to hang upside down. But all to no avail. Not a word was spoken.

And he continued to remain bald.

Then one day a wandering dervish happened to pass by. He was dressed in a sackcloth and he was bareheaded in more ways than one, for on his head there was neither a turban or for that matter any hair. The dervish was as bald as the outside of a basin or a bowl. The perfumer's shop made no impression on the dervish, for he neither had the desire nor the money to buy any scents. As for the mêlée of people milling around the shop's entrance, they too failed to attract his attention or interest.

But no sooner had the parrot spotted the wandering bald dervish did he liven up and in a loud voice he shrieked to the dervish:

'Hello there! Did you also spill oil from a bottle?'

In this way Rumi taught that we should not judge the actions of holy men by our own standards. The word 'sheer' in Persian means both milk and lion, but these two have as much in common as a careless parrot and a wandering dervish. One may come across two reeds in the water; one may be hollow inside, the other full of sugarcane. Both look exactly the same. In the same way bitter water and sweet water both look clear, but as Rumi points out, it takes someone who can taste to know the difference between that which is sweet and that which is not.

But that is not the end of the story.

The years passed and the parrot recovered his feathers and resumed his talking (though on some occasions, when he would not stop talking and passing comments on people in that sarcastic manner that Indian parrots have, his perfumer would wish for those weeks of silence). Together the two, the

shop owner and the bird, would daily sit on the bench outside their shop, for the parrot seemed convinced that he owned half the shop, and the perfumer was too generous to contradict him and wise enough to know that parrots had no legal rights, at least not in Baghdad (he had checked with a lawyer who was married to his sister — one can never be too sure). Things seemed as they were except for one difference: the perfumer, unwilling to lose any more oil, now placed the parrot in a bird cage.

Now, it was the perfumer's custom to travel once a year to India to trade in scents, for it was there that the most aromatic and enticing perfumes could be bought. He now generously asked all his friends:

'Tell me quickly what I should bring for you, and I shall bring it. What is it that you desire?'

Each of them asked for a thing much desired and the perfumer gave his promise to all. Then he turned to the parrot, for it was on a previous trip to India that he had bought him:

'And you, my dear friend, Baghbagh (for though the parrot detested it as much as he detested the cardamoms that children sometimes forced him to eat, that was the name that his owner had chosen for him), what present would you like me to bring you from your homeland?'

For a while the parrot remained silent, then in a solemn voice he replied:

'When you see the parrots there in the land of my fathers, tell them about my state. Tell them that Baghbagh sends his greetings to his cousins and regrets that, having been taken away from the land to which he belongs, he is unable to join you.'

The perfumer was taken aback both by the words that the parrot had spoken and by the eloquence with which he had uttered them, but being a man of his word, he promised that the message would be delivered.

And so things came to pass that the perfumer reached India safely and concluded his business profitably. Then it was time to buy the gifts that had been requested of him, and he was not ungenerous in doing so. Finally all his promises had been fulfilled except for the one he had made to Baghbagh, and so he travelled to the remotest region in India where he tracked down a number of parrots who were perched on a tree. The man halted his horse and greeted the parrots and the parrots returned his greeting, for parrots in India are exceedingly polite. The man then conveyed Baghbagh's message word for word.

Upon hearing the message one of the parrots, the one nearest the perfumer, began to tremble and fell from the tree to the ground where it lay motionless — to all purposes dead.

The perfumer blanched with terror. What had he said to cause such pain and anguish in so gentle a bird?

'What made me do this? Why did I deliver the message? My words have slain this noble bird!'

There was nothing left to say, and so the perfumer took his leave with a solemn farewell and soon he began his journey back to Baghdad which he reached in safety. He was happy to be back, for his business had gone well and he had missed his family and friends. He had also missed Baghbagh and it was to his shop that he first headed; and he could barely contain his smile when he saw his friend in a cage, pacing eagerly up and down awaiting his master's return.

A few hours later when the man had rested, Baghbagh asked him:

'Tell me all that you said and all that you saw!'

'No' replied the merchant, 'I regret passing your message to your friends. It caused nothing but pain. Why did I, in my ignorance, pass such a crude message?'

But the parrot insisted that he be told everything, and the perfumer eventually relented and spoke.

'I recounted all your complaints to an assembly of parrots very much like yourself. When I had finished speaking, one of the parrots began to tremble and then fell to the ground, where it lay motionless and dead to the world.'

Baghbagh listened gravely to his owner's words and then nodded to himself, as if a great and important message had been passed on. The perfumer shrugged to himself. He could never understand those parrots, with their green plumage and their love of sugar. They all seemed so moody. Soon he was distracted by business matters, and for the rest of the day he remained in the shop tending to his affairs.

It was not until an hour or so before evening, as the heat of the day was finally easing and a gentle breeze began to cool the city, that the perfumer went to rest on the bench outside his shop. But when he got there what he saw caused him to cry out in alarm. His parrot Baghbagh was lying at the bottom of the cage, dead!

'Baghbagh' he cried out, 'what has happened to you?' But he got no response, and in terror the perfumer threw open the cage door. And no sooner had he done that, than in a flash did Baghbagh, to his owner's amazement and wonderment, fly straight out of the cage. Twice he circled around the shop before stopping to rest on a branch of a tree that shaded the bench on which the perfumer and Baghbagh had sat for many years.

'It is time for me to return to where I come from' Baghbagh now told his owner. 'For years I have been in this cage, and it is a beautiful cage. You have treated me well, and the sugar that you fed me was both delicious and plentiful. But we are not born to live in cages.'

'But I don't understand,' the puzzled perfumer pondered, 'why did you pretend to die?'

'For years I lived in this beautiful cage,' replied the parrot, 'and I thought happiness was a piece of sugar. But deep inside me I knew that I had not been brought to this earth simply to eat sugar. My problem was that I had lost my way. I no longer knew the path home. And so when I heard that you were going to India, I pleaded with you to deliver my message in the hope that I could find an answer to my dilemma.'

'But when I delivered your message' the owner stammered, 'all that happened was that one of the parrots fell to the ground dead!'

'And that was the message! Die before you die. It is only by dying to the beauty of the bird cage and the taste of the sugar that I could find my way home.'

'But...but I don't understand. Does that mean that the parrot in India was only pretending to die? Was he passing you a message?'

But the parrot had spoken enough, and with a mischievous wink and a final farewell, he flew off heading for home.

'Die before you die!' The words that Rumi put in the parrot's mouth are from a very important saying of the Prophet Muhammad (ﷺ). We are all born to die, for death is something that no one can avoid even if we tried to flee from it to the very ends of the earth.

In another story, 'Solomon and the Angel of Death,' Rumi shows us the truth of that statement.

*'For years I lived in this beautiful cage,'
replied the parrot, 'and I thought
happiness was a piece of sugar!'*

Solomon and The Angel of Death

One day, into the court of the great king Solomon rushed a nobleman. On his face was an expression of such terror that the only possible explanation was that he had seen the Angel of Death himself, which in fact he had.

The man's face was pale from anguish, and his trembling lips had turned blue from fear. His knees shook to such an extent that, had it not been for the poor man's tortured expression, Solomon's guards would have simply assumed that he had imbibed too much Shirazi wine and flung him out of the palace, turban first. But a glance at the man's eyes told them that drink had not caused this state of anguish. They allowed him to approach Solomon, although twice they had to prevent him from falling, for his very legs kept giving way.

'Seat this poor man and give him water!' Solomon's voice thundered cross the court, 'for any man can clearly see that a great calamity has befallen him.'

And when the man had reposed for a few minutes and had been partly soothed by the water and by some fruit sorbet, kept cold by snow brought from the mountains of Lebanon, Solomon asked him what possible vision could have caused such terror.

'My King, it was none other than Azrael!' the man spluttered.

'Azrael himself?' asked Solomon.

'The Angel of Death himself. I saw him as I now see you.' The man then explained that a few hours earlier he had been seated at home in the midst of some friends, when lo and behold, someone or something on his left attracted his attention. 'And when I glanced over, my liege,' the man continued, 'it was none other than Azrael.'

Solomon remained silent, for he was not only a king but a prophet as well, and he understood fully that Azrael's visit could only mean one thing.

'But,' the man continued, 'that is not all. When Azrael looked at me, he seemed … he seemed puzzled!'

'Puzzled?'

'Yes my King, puzzled.'

A murmur now spread across Solomon's court, for all the nobles present were transfixed by what they were hearing. 'Puzzled? How could an Angel appear so?' they enquired of each other. Though as they did so all eyes were on Solomon, for surely he with all his famed wisdom would explain what possible earthly matter could puzzle the Angel of Death.

'My friend.' Solomon's words immediately silenced all talk. 'You have been blessed in ways immeasurable. Few people are given the opportunity to learn of their impending death, though death could come to any of us in the next second. You now have time to pay your debts and bid farewell to your family: but grieve not, for you will surely meet them again in paradise. So prepare in prayer to meet your Lord. That is all that I have to say.'

But the man was not listening to Solomon's words. 'My liege, many years ago, you recall, when I was in your service, you told me that you would grant me any wish. Surely, my liege, you recall that?'

'I do recall it.' For the man had spoken the truth.

Many years ago this nobleman had rendered a great service to Solomon when he had helped defeat a terrible enemy. And such was the valour of the

nobleman's actions that Solomon had, in the aftermath of the victorious battle, granted him any wish that he desired. At that time the man had remained silent, and the years had passed. But clearly he had not forgotten, for one never forgets the promise made by a king.

'Well, now I request that you order the wind that is under your command to transport me at once to India!'

'And there you believe you may flee from the Angel of Death?' Solomon's voice could barely conceal his incredulity.

'Yes, my King.'

'Listen to me. When God sends suffering the spiritually weak react by fleeing from God; the lovers of God react by moving closer to Him. In battle all fear death, but the cowards choose to retreat while the brave charge toward the enemy. Fear carries the courageous forward, but the weak spirited die in themselves. Suffering and fear are touchstones: they distinguish the brave from the cowards.

For many years you have ridden and fought by my side. You have seen countless men struck down in the heat of battle. Men who barely a few minutes earlier had roared like lions with life, lying by the dozen, lifeless, their souls departed to a better place. You, of all people, have witnessed first hand the frailty of life, and how easily the string that attaches us to this

earthly form that we inhabit can be cut. My friend, listen to me, for I speak to you not just as your king who demands your loyalty but as your prophet who prays for your salvation. Prepare for your death. Pray for mercy.

Everyone is so frightened of death,
But the true Sufis just laugh:
Nothing overpowers their hearts.
What strikes the oyster shell does not harm the pearl.

But the man's mind was too anxious and his soul too anguished to listen to Solomon's words, and he insisted that his wish be granted.

'I have been told that when a king gives his word he is too generous to ask for it back!' The man's words were uttered with a challenging, almost disrespectful tone, that at another time would have seen him arrested. But the guards remained still, for everyone — save this seemingly demented, anguished soul — knew that the Angel of Death never paid social visits.

'So be it!' Solomon sat back in his throne, 'So be it.' He now commanded the winds to transport the man over the oceans and hills to the depths of Hindustan. And to the astonishment of everyone a fierce wind began to howl through the court, lifted the man off his feet and, in the blink of an eye, carried him out of the window.

Later, when he was on his own, Solomon summoned Azrael into his presence. The Prophet Solomon greeted the Angel of Death and then told him about the man who had so foolishly tried to escape his destiny.

'But tell me one thing,' he enquired of Azrael, 'why did you look so puzzled when you saw this man?'

'I was puzzled' replied Azrael, 'because only this morning I was told by Our Lord that I should take this man's soul, and that this soul would be found in Hindustan. And as you well know as a prophet, that which is written in the Book cannot be unwritten. And yet, on my way I happened to pass by a house and on glancing inside, to my astonishment I spotted the very same man whose soul I was meant to take in Hindustan. Except that he was here in Jerusalem! Now, I have seen many things. I have been offered gold and jewels by desperate men and women not to take their souls, to return later after they had said goodbye to their loved ones, unaware that the Beloved was awaiting them. Would you keep the King waiting to say goodbye to the footman? Gold and jewels! If only man could see that the greatest gold is prayer and the most precious jewel fasting. But I have never seen', the Angel of Death continued, 'a man whose soul was meant to be in Hindustan staring at me in Jerusalem. Even if he had a hundred wings it would be impossible for him to reach the lands of India in one day. That is why I am puzzled.'

'Puzzle no more,' replied Solomon, 'for that which written is writ. The soul which you seek is indeed in Hindustan.'

From the minute that we enter this life the moment of our death is decreed, so explained Rumi. Be it in Hindustan or Jerusalem, in a few minutes or in a hundred years, no man can escape from his destiny. What is decreed is decreed, and there is nothing more to say. Nothing in life is more certain than death.

But if death is certain for every man, then equally certain is the meeting with God on the Day of Judgement. We are put on this earth for one purpose and one purpose only — to worship God with all our heart and all our mind and all our soul. If we do so then the attractions of the world, though beautiful in their way, will not distract us from our purpose. That is what the Prophet Muhammad (ﷺ) said when he urged his Companions to 'die before you die'. The second death is followed by Judgement and then, to those who are blessed, by Paradise. But Paradise can also be tasted here below by those who do not allow the world to distract them, as Rumi often reminds us in his writings.

There is one thing in this world that must never be forgotten. If you were to forget everything else but did not forget that, then there would be no cause to worry. Whereas if you performed and remembered and did not forget anything else, but forgot that one thing, then you would have done nothing whatsoever.

It is just as if a king had sent you to another country to carry out a specified task. You go and perform a hundred other tasks, but if you have

not performed that particular task it is as though you have done nothing at all. You have come into this world for a particular task and that is your purpose; if you do not perform it, then you will have done nothing.

Chapter 2

As the son of a famous scholar, Rumi's education was bound to be thorough. To tutor his son, Baha ud-Din appointed a man by the name of Burhan ud-Din at whose feet Rumi sat every day. The first things the young Rumi studied were the Qur'an and Hadith. Then he would have begun the study of Fiqh (Islamic Law) and his first lesson would have been on ablution. Then came prayer: how and when to perform it. He would then learn about Zakat, about fasting and pilgrimage. He would be taught the laws of barter and sale, debt and inheritance. Following that Rumi would be instructed on the laws of marriage and divorce, followed by those on crime and violence. But even that was not the end of the matter, and he would also have to learn both Arabic and Persian grammar as well as mathematics, logic, physics, metaphysics, politics, astronomy and philosophy! Rumi was undoubtedly a brilliant student, dazzling everyone with the speed of his learning. Why else would his father refer lovingly to his young son as Mawlana (our teacher)? The title would stick, and henceforth Rumi has been known as Mawlana (Mevlana in Turkish) Rumi.

The Two Bear-Hunters

One day two old friends, Ali and Hasan, went out to hunt a bear. Now, it was at least a three day journey to where the bears lived, so the two friends packed enough food for the journey and set off early one day at dawn. At the end of each day they would unpack their food and light a fire, and as they ate they would talk about how they would spend the money that they would get when they sold the bearskin in the market.

'I am not sure whether I should buy a couple of mules for my farm,' mused Ali, 'Or maybe I should really repair the roof on my house. Every time it rains, the water drips in and my wife won't speak to me for at least four days.'

'No. No. No!' replied Hasan, 'Mules? Why are you talking about mules? Is that what you aspire to be? A mule owner? As for your roof, let the water drip! And if your wife does not speak to you, well, my friend you should consider that a blessing! Do you not always complain about how she nags you endlessly? No! You should spend your money on more exciting things. As for me, I am going to buy a race horse, the best money can buy. And the speed of that horse will make me famous, so that wherever I go I will be courted as the owner of the fastest horse in the East. Or maybe I will travel to Baghdad and Isfahan and Shiraz and …'

'A horse!' retorted his travelling companion. 'Pray tell me what a horse is if not a mule with pretensions. You are deluded, you see a mule can …'

And so it went on — for the first day, and for the second and for the third. The days were spent heading to where the bears lived, and the nights in earnest discussion on how the two men would spend their hard-earned money.

Soon the land of the bears loomed ahead and the talking became less, for their prey was not far off now.

'We will rest here for a while next to this big tree before we continue any further.' Soon the two men were fast asleep, for the journey had not been easy and the nights had been spent in long discussions on how the money would be spent. And so it came to pass, that within minutes, under the shade of the tree, soothed by a cool breeze that rustled the leaves, the men fell into a deep sleep.

It was not long before the men's appearance in the jungle had been noticed by the animals, for the spices in the food that they had brought with them could hardly fail to attract their attention. The sense of smell in certain animals is highly developed, and none more so than in bears.

Now, as it turned out a bear happened to be in the area, which is not surprising given the fact that this was the land where bears lived. What was perhaps more noteworthy was that this particular bear was not a happy one. The reason why he was not happy is too long and complicated to go into, and all that we need to know is never to ask an unhappy bear why he is unhappy.

To fall asleep in the land of the bears is either an extremely brave or extremely foolhardy thing to do. To continue to sleep as these two men did, while an unhappy bear is towering over them, is just making the Angel of Death's task easier, for at least the man in the earlier story had tried to flee to Hindustan.

'How strange these humans are,' the bear reflected (part of his unhappiness, his parents often told him, was that he reflected too much. Bears shouldn't reflect, they repeated, they should hunt). 'How strange. What other animal would just lie there in the open, totally unprotected, so certain of their superiority over the other animals? Look at them! On their backs, their mouths open!'

It wasn't the first time he had seen humans, of course, but for the life of him he could never figure out why they considered themselves to be so intelligent. They made so much noise when they walked and they smelled so badly. But that was not the worst part. No, the worst part was that they talked incessantly! Talk, talk, talk! What subjects could possibly be so interesting to keep their jaws so busy. Did they not know that silence was necessary to be able to listen out for danger? Didn't their mothers teach them that when they were babes? Clearly not, otherwise they wouldn't be lying down under the tree snoring away. They couldn't even run very fast. All they did was come to the jungle and hunt animals. Animals like his friends the deer, or the fish, or the … or the bears. Yes! Bears like himself who had done them no harm whatsoever. By now the bear was getting even unhappier than he had been before. No! It was time to teach those humans a lesson they would not easily forget.

And so, gently approaching the two sleeping men (didn't these humans have any sense of danger?), the bear unleashed the most ferocious, bloodcurdling growl that he could muster. Now, one must understand that in animal speech, a bear's growl can mean many things, and this particular one meant: 'Here are two humans who have come to hunt us down. Let's have some fun with them!' And as the growl echoed off the trees, a lion who had happened to be passing by stood still for a few seconds and shook his head sadly. He knew, as all animals knew, that God had created man as His noblest creature, superior to the animals, even the lions, but for the life of him he could not understand why. Surely God could not have meant those two, fast asleep under the tree.

For human ears, though, a bear's growl meant only one thing, and the two terrified men sat bolt upright in sheer terror from their sleep and their dreams of wealth to find towering over them a bear so enormous that he blocked out the sun. Somehow, though how he managed to do it he had no idea, Ali leapt to his feet and clambered up the tree as fast as he possibly could, until he found himself on the top branch. As for poor Hasan, his legs refused to obey him, and he lay there staring up helplessly at the unhappy bear. Slowly and ominously the bear approached Hasan and leant over him so closely that their faces almost touched. Then to the amazement of Ali, who was watching in terror as his friend seemed about to be devoured, the bear appeared to whisper something into Hasan's ear before stepping away and walking off with what seemed like, and in fact was, total disdain for the two terrified human beings.

For a long time neither Ali nor Hasan moved. For some reason the bear had spared them, even though he could have killed them both so easily. Then, when he was certain that the bear had gone for good, Ali climbed down and helped his friend to his feet, and the two beat as hasty a retreat as they could. All that was on their minds now was to get back to the safety of the city as quickly as possible.

'But tell me,' Ali asked his friend when both men had somehow regained their ability to speak, 'it seemed to me that the bear whispered something to you. Could that be possible?'

'He did, indeed.'

'But pray tell me, what did he say?'

Hasan shook his head sadly. 'He told me, *don't sell the bear-skin before you have hunted the bear!'*

Now, as we have seen, Ali and Hasan were friends; and although friendship between people is a noble and good thing, and though it is possible for a man to befriend an animal or a bird, like the perfumer and the parrot, it is extremely inadvisable, as our next story clearly demonstrates, for a man to befriend a bear or for a bear to befriend a man.

But in this story the bear was certainly wiser than our two friends. For the bear knew that too much talk was a waste of time, and never more so than idle talk about making money or buying things before you have actually got the money in your hand. Like most things in your life, it is better to be grateful for what you have and then make the intention to achieve something more rather than speak endlessly about something which you have not yet achieved: 'don't sell the bear-skin before you have hunted the bear!'

Beware of Befriending a Bear

One day a man was passing through a forest when he came across a terrible and fearsome commotion. Ahead of him a dragon was in combat with a bear. The poor bear was getting a terrible beating and would surely perish if the man did not intervene. And so the man, who was certainly brave if somewhat foolhardy, drew out his sword, and charging at the dragon, managed to slay it with one fierce blow. The bear, now safe, retreated to lick its wounds, and had the man continued on his journey all would have been well. However, the man did not continue for the time being, but instead decided to befriend the bear, who was happy to reciprocate the friendship. And so the man and the bear became friends and set out on the journey together. Since the bear knew the forest better, the man followed him quite happily. At night, when the man slept, the bear would keep watch and protect him from any threat, while during the day the two would march in

silence, for they had little to say to each other.

After a few days travel the man and the bear came across some farmers ploughing their land at the edge of the forest. No sooner did the farmers see the two approach than they ran away in terror, but the man smiled at them and urged them not to be afraid.

'Do not fear.' He told the men, 'he is a gentle bear whom I have saved from a dragon. He will not harm you.'

But the farmers would not listen. As they fled one of them shouted out:

'Gentle or not, he is a bear. That is his nature. A man and a bear should not be friends. It is not in the nature of things.'

But the man would not listen. After all, the bear seemed harmless, even friendly. Why should a man and a bear not be friends? Had he not guided him safely through the forest and protected him while he slept?

Now, it was a particularly hot day and the man decided to nap for a while before continuing the journey. The bear, as was his custom, stood guard over his friend who had saved him from the dragon. The heat of the day meant that flies were plentiful and the bear kept driving them away, but despite his efforts they soon returned. When this had happened several times, the bear became furious (bears are notoriously short-tempered) and headed for a

nearby hill where he picked up a large rock. Returning with the rock, he noticed that the flies had settled on the man's sleeping face.

Out of friendship he flung the rock at the flies to scare them away, and in doing so crushed the poor man to death.

Good bears, no matter how good their intentions, can not be like good humans — and vice versa. The nature of beings can only change as far as Nature allows. Ultimately all of us are confined to striving to be the best that we can be — within the limits of our True nature.

Chapter 3

In the year 1219 Rumi's father Baha ud-Din took his family and hastily departed from Balkh in order to flee from the advancing Mongol threat. His first stop was the fabled city of Nishapur where he introduced Rumi, who was twelve years old, to the great mystical poet Farid ud-Din Attar, author of the famous poem 'The Conference of the Birds'. Attar, we are told, was greatly taken by Rumi and gave him a copy of his 'Book of Secrets', predicting somewhat enigmatically that Rumi would soon light a fire in the hearts of all mystic lovers. As for Rumi, he held a deep affection for Attar throughout his life, and used to say that Attar 'has crossed the seven cities of Love, whereas I am still at the corner of a narrow street.'

Eventually, after much travelling, Baha ud-Din settled his family in the city of Konya, where he had been invited by its Sultan to teach. And so for the first time the name of Konya appears in our story, never to leave it; for, apart from some years spent travelling, Rumi would live there for the remainder of his life. No city in Islam, with the notable and blessed exception of Medina, is so linked with one person, so that whenever the name of Konya is mentioned we always think of Rumi.

The Teacher & the Bear

It is time to return to our unhappy bear and to the reason for his unhappiness. Now, though some bear therapists have pointed to his excessive love for honey, and though his parents, as we have seen, felt that it was his tendency to reflect too much, he himself would probably trace the roots of his gloom to the day when he was floating down the river minding his own business.

A schoolteacher, we read in one of Rumi's stories, who was so utterly destitute that he had only a cotton shirt to wear, was standing near a flowing river when he suddenly saw a bear in the water. To the teacher and the schoolchildren around him it seemed that the animal had fallen into the gushing waters and was being carried downstream by the current. The schoolchildren, pitying their teacher, told him to jump into the river and seize the fine fur coat which would keep him warm in the winter.

'When it dries it will be a fine coat and keep you warm for many winters.'

Out of despair, for the cold was bitter and winter was barely in its infancy, the teacher listened to the children and leapt into the water and tried to seize the fur coat, only to come across our unhappy bear (except, of course, until then he had been rather jolly), who often floated down the river as he found the currents an excellent massage for his painful back.

Now picture the scene: a jolly bear (with a painful back) minding his own business, floating gently down a river, eyes shut to the world, lost in thought. When out of nowhere, a demented half-naked man lands on top of him (urged on from the bank by a group of shrieking children — how he detested children!) and starts to pull at his skin! Of course he was not scared, not even alarmed, for it would take more than a semi-clothed madman to harm him. So rather than swat him away like a fly, he simply grabbed him to his chest and gently carried him down the river.

To the horrified children on the bank, however, it seemed as if their teacher was locked in mortal combat, and they all cried out in one voice:

'Let the fur coat go!'

To this the teacher plaintively replied: 'I have let the fur coat go, but the

fur coat won't let me go!'

In this way Rumi notes that once love of God has grasped you it will never let you go! Our desire for God, writes Rumi, is fanned by His love; it is His attraction that draws all wayfarers along the path. Does the dust rise up without the wind? Does a ship float without a sea? Elsewhere Rumi tells us about the person who asked God: 'What is love?' God answered: 'You will know when you lose yourself in Me.' We may think that we have got hold of the fur skin, but in reality the fur skin has got hold of us. A lover never seeks without being sought by his beloved. When the love of God grows in your heart, notes Rumi, beyond any doubt God loves you. While the thirsty seek water, the water also seeks the thirsty.

But there is no way of understanding the ways of God intellectually. A child loves milk and gathers strength from it, but is unable to explain it or to describe it precisely. He cannot express the pleasure he has in drinking it or how miserable he would be if he was deprived of it. It is simply that his soul is in love with the milk and desires it intensely. At the same time, a theologian can explain milk in a thousand ways but not enjoy it. To explain this further, Rumi related the story of the Sultan and his idiot son.

Does the dust rise up without the wind?
Does a ship float without a sea?

The Sultan & his Idiot Son

Many years ago, there once ruled a mighty Sultan whose power and wealth knew no bounds. The city's treasuries were full to the brim with gold, silver and jewels, all brought in as a result of victories on the battlefields achieved by a fierce and invincible army. As for the city itself, peace and prosperity reigned throughout, for the Sultan ensured that the people had food for their families and that the city walls were secure from enemy attack.

And yet, as is often the case in the world, the Sultan was unhappy and restless. And if one were to enquire as to the cause (except that of course no one in his court would dare ask the Sultan anything), he would have eagerly responded (since he hated the sullen silences which infested his court, and often wished that someone would actually ask a question) that the cause of his anxiety was the education of his son, the future Sultan, or to be precise, his lack of education.

The fact of the matter was that the Sultan's son was, to put it mildly and as delicately as possible, not intelligent. In his father's presence, he would be described by the Viziers and their Ministers in flowery terms such as 'innocent as a spring day,' 'fresh to the problems of the world', 'he views life with a striking simplicity,' 'he refuses to allow complicated issues to bother him,' and so on. But in the absence of the Sultan the words were more frank, such as 'he is as dumb as the dumbest mule from Basra who has been left out in the sun for too long — only dumber.'

The problem, therefore, was a basic one, as was the solution — or so thought the Sultan who, befitting his position, never came across a problem which he could not resolve.

'Find me the best teachers who reside in my empire,' he growled.

At once soldiers were sent out to scour the mosques, madrasas and colleges in the cities and villages scattered in the north of the empire, and in the east, in the west, and in the south. And in each city and village the soldiers would ask: 'Who is your greatest teacher?' When they were told that so and so was the best grammarian, theologian or mathematician in that particular district, the soldiers would drag him or her off to Baghdad.

In this way the greatest minds ever assembled in the history of Islam found themselves gathered in the presence of the Sultan, who explained to them that the task that lay ahead of them was perhaps the hardest and most arduous which they would ever face. They needed to turn his idiot of a son into a scholar. No subject in Heaven or on earth would be spared him, from astronomy to rhetoric, from theology to geometry.

'You are all teachers — the best in your fields,' he reasoned. 'Here you have a student who needs to be taught. So teach!'

Now, the Sultan told the scholars that he fully understood that he could not force them to remain in Baghdad, that he was certain they all had very important unfinished manuscripts to return to, and that he could only request it of them. And when all present readily agreed to tutor the young man to the best of their abilities, the Sultan smiled and became reassured that here, indeed, were the most intelligent of his subjects, for only the subtlest of minds could work out the difference between a royal request and an order.

And so the months turned into years, the old tutors died and the young ones grew old teaching the Sultan's son. Every day, from dawn till dusk, poetry was recited, mathematical formulae memorised, legal points taken apart, manuscripts pored over, and theological points pondered. All the while the anxious Sultan would be reassured by even more anxious and increasingly perplexed tutors (for truly the young man was a marvel in imbecility),

'He is learning, my liege. He is nearly a scholar.'

Finally the day came when the Sultan was informed by one of the exhausted scholars that there did not exist a single subject under the sun which his son had not studied and mastered. The task which had been set had been met, and the Sultan's son had been transformed into a scholar.

Relieved but suspicious, the Sultan now asked for his son, who shortly afterwards stumbled into the Royal chamber dressed in the most elegant scholar's gown and turban, and carrying under each arm two heavy manuscripts.

'My son,' the Sultan exclaimed, 'my heart leaps with joy at the sight of you as a scholar with all that wisdom which you have been taught. But let me test you.' Then, turning his back to his son, the Sultan took off his green emerald ring and held it in his fist.

'Tell me my learned scholar. What am I holding in my hand?'

To the Sultan's astonishment, his son replied confidently, 'You are holding something which is round and green.' It was a miracle! Truly the teachers had performed a wondrous task in transforming his son into a scholar.

'Since you have given all the signs correctly,' the Sultan said, glowing with pride, 'now pronounce what thing it is'.

'Well,' his son answered, 'since it is round and green, it must be a water-melon.'

'What?' cried the King, 'You correctly understood all the minute signs in a manner which would baffle the greatest minds, and which is a reflection of the tremendous education that you have received; but out of all your powerful learning and knowledge, how can it be possible that this one small point should have escaped you: that a watermelon cannot be contained in a fist?'

In this way Rumi explained that the great scholars of the age may have studied all manner of sciences and have a complete comprehension of matters great and small, but as for what truly matters, the one thing that touches a man more closely than all else — his inner self, his heart, his love of God — of this the great scholar remains unaware. He may pronounce with great authority on what is legal or otherwise, claiming authoritatively, 'This is permitted and that is not. This is lawful and that is not.' He may measure the distance between the moon and the earth, and he may even calculate with unfailing accuracy the most detailed points of geometry. But if asked to account for the purity of his self or his heart, then all the books he has studied and all the manuscripts over which he has pored will not come to his aid, for in the face of this eternal question books cannot tell the difference between an emerald ring and a watermelon. He knows the precise value of every article he buys and sells, but in his folly he does not know his own value. He has learned to distinguish auspicious stars from inauspicious ones, but he does not examine his own soul to see if he is in a fortunate or poor spiritual state.

To know yourself, Rumi stresses, is to master the highest science.

'So does that mean that books and scholarship are pointless?' Rumi was often asked, and he answered that the words found in a book were useful for the sake of that person who is in need of words in order that he may understand. 'But as for the man who understands without words,' he asks us, 'what need has he of words?'

How can it be possible that this one small point should have escaped you: that a watermelon cannot be contained in a fist?

Does the Sultan Speak Arabic?

Now, the very same Sultan who sought in vain to transform his son into a scholar was himself of Turkish origin and spoke no Arabic. So when it came to pass that one day an Arabic-speaking poet visited Baghdad and asked for a Royal audience in order to recite his latest poem, the Sultan's vizier agreed, since he thought that no harm would come out of it.

And so the following day the Arab poet entered into the Royal Chamber and respectfully bowed to the Sultan, who had taken his seat on the throne. And when the vizier, the commanders and the ministers had all taken their places, the poet began to recite his poem. And then a remarkable thing happened. At every passage meriting applause the Sultan nodded his head in admiration, while at every passage provoking astonishment he looked amazed. No one could believe it! The vizier, the commanders and the ministers were all astounded.

'Our Sultan does not speak Arabic' they murmured amongst each other, 'and yet he seemed to understand every word the poet was saying. He must have known Arabic all these years and kept it from us.' And when they had thus spoken, they became increasingly worried as they recalled the many occasions when they had spoken to each other in Arabic in the presence of the Sultan, assuming that he understood not a jot of what they said.

For a few days the ministers and courtiers fretted and worried, until it was agreed amongst them that they had to find out whether the Sultan did or did not understand Arabic. Now, the Sultan had a favourite slave, and the ministers went to him and gave him many gifts, including a horse and a mule and a sum of money, and urged him to find out the answer to the question which was tormenting them.

'Just inform us whether or not the Sultan knows Arabic,' they pleaded. 'If he does not, then how was it that he nodded just at the right places? Was it a miracle? Was it divine inspiration?'

The slave agreed to find out and watched his master closely; but not once did he detect any sign that the Sultan understood even a single word of Arabic. By now the slave, too, had become equally intrigued by the Sultan's miraculous understanding of Arabic poetry, when it was clear that he neither spoke nor understood a word of the language.

Finally, one day while hunting with his master, the slave could hold himself back no longer, and perceiving that the Sultan was in good humour, he explained to him the court's astonishment and asked him openly whether he understood Arabic.

Upon hearing this the Sultan burst out laughing.

'By Allah, I neither speak nor understand Arabic,' he said. 'As for my nodding and applauding, I knew of course what the poet's object was in reciting the poem. What other subject do you think a poet would choose in the presence of the Sultan except his praise? And so I nodded and applauded whenever there was a silence.'

Rumi thus explained to his disciples that they should not allow words or books to distract them from the object in view. The poem itself was merely the branch of that object. If it had not been for that object the poet would never have composed the poem. And so it is with scholars who write books. The object needs to be kept in view, and that object can be none other than God. If it is, then whether the branch of the book be on astronomy or on trigonometry, the root is one.

But if the scholar were simply to look at the words written and view not the object behind the words, then his efforts would be fruitless. After all, the

Qur'an tells us: 'If the sea were ink for the Words of my Lord, the sea would be spent before the Words of my Lord are spent.'

And yet, Rumi pointed out, if one were to purchase fifty drams of ink, one can write out the whole of the Qur'an.

Chapter 4

It was in Konya that Rumi, under the guidance of his old teacher, Burhan ud-Din, became initiated into the spiritual ways of the Sufis. Then, in the year 1240, after seven years of guiding Rumi along the spiritual path and feeling that his teachings were completed, Burhan ud-Din told Rumi, 'You are now ready, my son. You have no equal in any of the branches of learning. You have become a lion of knowledge. I am such a lion myself, and we are not both needed here, and that is why I want to go. Furthermore,' he said mysteriously, 'a great friend will come to you and you will be each other's mirror. He will lead you to the innermost parts of the spiritual life, just as you will lead him. Each of you will complete the other, and you will be the greatest friends in the entire world.' With these enigmatic words, Burhan ud-Din departed from Konya and travelled to Kayseri, the ancient Caesarea, where he settled and where he died shortly afterwards. His modest tomb, surrounded by flowers and still visited, lies in an old cemetery above which rises Erciyes, the snow covered mountain .

For the next four years Rumi continued to teach law and religious sciences at the madrasa. His career as a teacher seemed assured until one day in October 1244 on his way home, he met a stranger who put a question to him, a question which was to transform Rumi's life to such an extent that it would not be an exaggeration to claim that it is with this fateful meeting the story of Rumi really begins. 'I was raw,' he wrote describing his life prior to this meeting, 'then I got cooked, and now I am burned.' Later he would elaborate on this. 'It is burning of the heart that I want. It is this burning which is everything, more precious than a worldly empire, because it calls God secretly, in the night.' The friend, of whom Burhan ud-Din had so enigmatically spoken, had finally arrived.

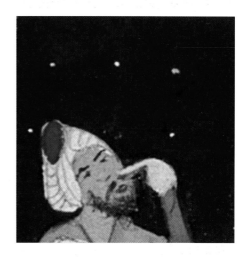

The Lost Merchant

This chapter begins with the story of a wealthy merchant on his way to the pilgrimage, when he got lost and found himself in the middle of a desert. It was a fiercely hot day, and the blazing sun meant that soon the man was overcome by a terrible thirst. Though the poor man looked to the left and to the right, though he strained his eyes to spot his travelling companions, he found himself lost and alone in the desert. Rapidly, as happens in the desert, he lost any sense of direction, and stumbling blindly, he had almost given up hope of any help. Suddenly, however, he espied on the horizon a small and tattered tent. Summoning up all his strength and energy he headed in that direction, and when he had approached the tent, he came across a woman. 'Help me!' he cried, 'I am lost and I need water. You are my only hope.'

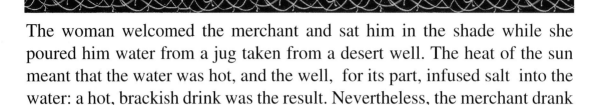

The woman welcomed the merchant and sat him in the shade while she poured him water from a jug taken from a desert well. The heat of the sun meant that the water was hot, and the well, for its part, infused salt into the water: a hot, brackish drink was the result. Nevertheless, the merchant drank his fill, glad that his thirst had been quenched, and grateful for the generosity of the woman.

When he had rested for a while, the merchant addressed the woman. 'I am grateful for the kindness that you have shown me,' he told her. 'You have saved my life, and I hope to repay you some of it back. I am a merchant and I travel frequently between Baghdad, Kufa and Wasit. Allah has blessed me with wealth and I have houses in all three cities. If you ever find your life here too harsh, then you and your family are my guests in any of my houses, where you will find plentiful sweet, cool water, foods of various kinds, baths, luxuries and other rich delights.' The merchant then spoke about life in those cities, the clothes that people wore, how they lived and travelled. To these words the woman listened, clearly transfixed, for she had never in her wildest imaginations ever thought such luxuries possible.

'And in the winter you have warm water to wash with?' she asked incredulously, and the merchant told her about the public baths scattered on the corners of every city, where hot water was in abundance.

'And you mentioned fruits,' the woman enquired. 'You mean to tell me you can choose which fruit to eat?' The merchant smiled gently, for the water,

though brackish, had revived his spirits. 'The markets are full of fruits gathered from every corner of the empire. Apricots and mangoes, berries and bananas, grapes and oranges.'

In this way the two talked until the merchant enquired as to the whereabouts of the woman's husband.

'He has gone out to hunt for our dinner,' she informed him, and insisted that he be their guest for the evening. Since the merchant was both tired and hungry, he readily accepted.

An hour or so later the woman's husband returned, and in his hand he was carrying the dinner which he had managed to catch — a brace of hairy desert rats which he gave to his wife to cook while he sat with the merchant. Once again the merchant thanked the man for his and his wife's kind hospitality, but his words of gratitude were waved away.

'It is the least we can do,' the man replied, 'for a guest is always welcome.'

Soon the meal was ready and the three sat down in front of a plate, the food on which consisted of a couple of desert rats that the man had returned with, and which his wife had cooked so furiously on a fire, that parts of the rats were singed while parts remained barely cooked. Never had the merchant been presented with a more unappetising meal; but since he could not possibly offend his hosts, who had been so kind and generous to share their

meal with him, and also partly because he was ravenously hungry, having not eaten all day, the merchant chewed on the tough, grainy and tasteless meat that was on offer, managing only to swallow it thanks to gulps of hot, brackish water.

The meal (thankfully) over, the man offered to accompany the merchant to the nearest city, an offer that the merchant gratefully accepted. But that would not be until the following morning. So that night, while the merchant slept outside the tent under a starry sky, the woman approached her husband and whispered to him.

'Did you not hear all the stories our guest had to tell?' And she repeated to her husband what the merchant had told her.

'Don't listen to these things,' her husband answered. 'There are many envious people in the world. When they see some folk enjoying ease and plenty they envy them and want to deprive them of their fortune.'

So it is with some people, Rumi explained. When, out of pure compassion advice is offered them, they scorn it and believe that it was spoken out of envy. But everyone is according to his nature.

> *The moon sheds light when all is dark;*
> *The dog's reaction is to bark.*
> *Is that the moon's fault? Tell me true:*
> *'Tis the dog's nature so to do.*

The Lion and the Hare

The time has come to return to the lion whom we left a few stories ago shaking his mane. From our brief glimpse of him we could tell he was not amused by the two human beings. The truth was he was an angry lion (what with an unhappy bear and an angry lion, that particular jungle was not the most peaceful of places), and there was, above all, one cause for his anger: human beings. The sons of Adam, as he often sneeringly called them. He had a good reason for not liking them — a very good reason. Many years ago when he was a cub, some human beings had come to the jungle where he lived with his family and had hunted down his parents. For what reason, he could not figure out. To kill to eat was one thing; after all that was the law of the jungle. But human beings did not eat lion meat, nor did they even try to. No, it seemed to him that they killed because they could, and that he could not understand, and it made him angry that he could not understand.

Now he too killed because he could, and though in his deepest nature he knew it was wrong to do so, he did not cease, such was his anger. Few animals that crossed his path were spared, and no human being ever was. He could not recall how many humans he had slain, nor did he particularly care. If they were foolish enough to cross his path then they were foolish enough to die. That day when he had heard the bear's growl, he had assumed that the two men had been slain. Later, when he had been informed that the bear had let them off, he had cursed him loudly (almost causing a fight), and had followed their trail until he reached the outskirts of the city, where he advanced no further; for though he may be angry, unlike the sons of Adam, he was not a fool.

No, this was an angry lion; and though he instinctively knew that he was the King of the Jungle, this was a king who ruled by fear and terror. All the animals in the jungle were terrified of the lion. Some, like the wise elephant, tried to understand his brutal actions.

'He had such a difficult childhood, you see,' he pondered in the way that only elephants can ponder. But he could afford to be generous in his sentiments; elephants are not easy to attack and kill. As for the deer, the foxes, the wolves, the gazelles and all the other animals, they had all had enough. Something had to be done.

'He kills everyone who crosses his path,' the fox complained angrily.

'Whether he eats them or not,' remarked the deer.

'He is a savage. A brute!' It was now the monkey's turn.

But when it came down to what could be done to stop this angry, violent lion, the animals were silent. For in reality nothing could be done. The lion was too strong, too fast, and too angry. And so, as often happens when a group that is in fear of its life meets, a decision was made that satisfied no one but was accepted by everyone. A delegation would be sent to the lion through which an offer would be made. Now, it would be pointed out to him that the animals understood his anger and that they had a proposal. If he would stop indiscriminately killing any animal that crossed his path, they would in turn offer him an animal a day to slaughter. This way his anger would be sated and fewer animals would be killed.

It was decided that the delegation to the lion would consist of three: the elephant, the wolf and the eagle, for all were in their own right kings, and though their lives were equally in danger, it was felt that the lion would at least listen to their proposal.

And he did listen, and to their surprise and their sad relief he accepted this bloody deal (for though he would never admit it, he too was tired of the bloodshed).

'So every day, when the sun is at its highest, you will send me an animal to kill?' he drawled in his languid style.

'That is correct,' the wolf replied solemnly.

'I accept your offer. But I must warn you: if ever you fail to honour your side of the bargain, I will exact a terrible vengeance. For every day that you fail to provide me with a sacrifice, I will slaughter one hundred animals.' Now, never in the history of the animal kingdom has one ever dared say that the elephant, wolf or eagle lacked courage, but on hearing those chilling words each one of them shivered with fear.

And so the bargain was kept, and every day an animal — a fox, a gazelle, a deer, a monkey and so on — would be sent on their way to slaughter. Some complained, but on the whole the animals accepted their lot, for they knew that their death would effectively mean that on that particular day at least there would be no more slaughter.

Until the day came when it was the turn of the hare to be sent, and as he bade his family adieu and set off to meet his executioner, his mind was thinking rapidly, for hares were not just quick on their feet, but also in their wits. Shortly before he reached the place where the lion awaited him, he sat down and thought and thought and thought, so that the sun had long passed its highest point by the time he had stopped thinking. But by then it did not matter, for the hare knew exactly what he had to do.

By the time the hare reached the location where daily the animals met their deaths, fumes of anger were drifting slowly from the lion. But angry as he was, the lion was equally curious as to why this hare had made him wait.

'You are late.'

'I nearly didn't make it.' The hare's reply was calm and measured. 'We were attacked on the way.'

'We?' By now the lion was getting less angry and more curious. 'Who is "we"?'

'Well, those who sent me did not think that someone of your stature would be satisfied with just one small skinny hare. They sent two, so that your appetite is satisfied.'

'So where is your companion?'

'Well, we were on our way and the sun had not reached its height, when suddenly we were set upon by … by a …'

'A what? Don't tell me it was that scoundrel of a tiger,' growled the lion. 'I'll kill him! Or maybe it was that rascal leopard. I'll maim him! Or maybe it was that fiendish …'

'It was a lion,' the hare interrupted him (perhaps for the first time in the history of the animal kingdom a hare interrupted a lion).

'A lion?'

'A lion.'

'A lion?' The lion blinked twice, clearly puzzled.

'A lion.'

'But I am a lion. A LION? YOU ARE NOT TELLING ME …' by now the lion was roaring in anger and fury,

'Yes, there is another lion,' and for the second time the hare interrupted the lion (clearly he was a very brave hare).

By now the lion was pacing up and down in anger. 'How dare he! Who does he think he is? Does he not know that I am the King of the Jungle.' Then suddenly he stopped.

'So what does he look like, this lion?'

'He is very big and ferocious. When he saw us coming in this direction he blocked our path, snatched my companion, and dragged him to the well.

I had to run very fast to escape him. He was very scary.'

'Scary? I AM THE ONE WHO IS SCARY!' and such was the force of the lion's roar that the hare's ears flew back in the wind that was caused. 'I will not stand for this! I will kill him! Show me where the well is.'

And so the lion and the hare set off in the direction of the well, the hare leading the way with the lion close on his heels.

'I'll kill him ... How dare he?' muttered the lion, getting angrier and angrier, until finally the two reached the well.

'Well, there he is,' the hare said.

'Where?' growled the lion, looking left and right.

'There! In the well.'

'In the well?' The lion's eyes narrowed, and he now stared suspiciously at the hare. 'Are you trying to trick me? To push me down the well?'

'No, of course not,' replied the hare calmly, though his knees trembled with fear. 'I promise you he is down the well. Go and a have a look.'

'We will go together,' the lion declared. 'Step by step.'

So the two now proceeded slowly and somewhat cautiously towards the well and both peered into it. And, lo and behold, in the water they saw reflected an angry looking lion next to an anxious looking hare.

'Look! There he is!' the hare cried out. 'Quick, attack him before he kills us!'

'Kill us? Never!' shouted the lion whose anger had clouded his thinking, and he now leapt mane first into the well causing a great splash!

All this time the other animals in the jungle had been following the lion and hare, and they now rushed to the edge of the well and peered in. At its bottom lay the lion, now no longer angry, but looking hurt and broken of spirit.

'What shall we do?' the deer asked anxiously (deer tended to suffer from anxiety).

'Just leave him there!' stated the fox. 'He has caused us enough harm!'

'But look at him,' pointed the monkey as he clambered on the well's edge. 'He looks so helpless. What do you think, hare? After all, it was you who tricked him, and for that we are all grateful.'

'Yes, yes … grateful, grateful,' echoed all the animals, and they all now turned their eyes on the hare.

'I am not fit to answer this question,' the hare replied. 'I may be quick on foot and in wit, but it is not fitting that I speak and pass judgement when those who are superior to me are present. Elephant — you are wise; and in the absence of our King — for let us not forget though the lion who now lies at the bottom of the well, cruel as he may be, is our King — you assume his position.'

The elephant nodded solemnly, for he knew that the hare had spoken wisely and now it was his turn.

'The lion is our King. He has learnt this lesson so that each one of us may never forget it, to set us an example if you like, and for that we must be grateful.

'But what is that lesson?' the puzzled monkey asked.

'The lesson that all this anger, this hate, lies within us and is no one else's fault. He saw his anger reflected in the water and he thought it was some-one else, and so he attacked it. Despite his faults he is a noble king, and in attacking himself he showed us that we all have to attack the faults within us, and to blame no one else.'

The hare had been right, there was no disputing the wisdom of the elephant, and the animals now formed an animal chain down the well and dragged the drenched but grateful lion to the surface. Then, when the lion had rested for a while, he in his turn spoke.

'Forgive me for what I have done to you in the past, but I was blinded by anger and I blamed everyone but myself. Such was my fury that I could not even recognise myself reflected in the water.'

Each of the animals now hugged the lion, and all in their turn renewed his allegiance to him as King of the Jungle. All except for the unhappy bear, who turned up late.

'What happened! What's all the commotion? You will never guess where I have been. Can you imagine, there were these two hunters who were trying to hunt me and they fell asleep!'

All the animals now chuckled and laughed. How silly these sons of Adam were!

Despite his faults he is a noble king, and in attacking himself he showed us that we all have to attack the faults within us, and to blame no one else.

Chapter 5

We are told that Shams ud-Din Tabriz, who was aged about sixty when he met Rumi, had spent his life praying to God to let him meet one of His saints. We even read that Shams once vowed that he was prepared to give up his life in return for meeting a saint. We do not know whether the vow was accepted, but one night Shams dreamt that he should travel to Asia Minor, and to Konya in particular. He arrived in the city at the end of November 1244, where he stayed at inns normally occupied by sugar merchants. Then one day he spotted Rumi who was riding home from the madrasa on a mule and he knew that his prayers had been answered. At once Shams ran up, held the mule's bridle, and asked Rumi a question.

'What is the purpose of spiritual efforts?'

To this question Rumi, as a teacher of Religious Sciences, replied: 'To understand the traditions and the religious customs.'

'All this is external,' Shams retorted, much to the astonishment of Rumi's students, who had gathered to find out what all the commotion was about.

'And what is beyond traditions and religious customs?' Rumi enquired.

'The knowledge to cross from the unknown to the known.' Shams replied.

This is one version of the story of the first meeting of the two men. There are many other versions, but all end the same way. On hearing Shams's reply to his question, Rumi leapt off his mule and, to the great bewilderment of his students, fell at Shams's feet. There was no doubt; this was the friend of whom Burhan ud-Din had spoken.

Shams and Rumi became inseparable, so much so that Rumi's students justifiably complained that their teacher had neglected them completely. Soon it was not just the students but all the inhabitants of Konya who became shocked when they saw Rumi abandoning his social duties, and giving himself over completely to the company of this wandering dervish. When news of the people's displeasure reached the ears of Rumi he ignored it at first, and then tried to defend his friend. 'Men have left their own country,

their fathers and mothers, their households and kinsmen and families, and have journeyed from Hind to Sind, making boots of iron until they were cut to shreds, happily to encounter a man having the fragrance of the other world ... As for you, you have encountered such a man here in your own house, and you turn your back on him. This is surely a great calamity.'
Shams's arrival in Konya and his deep friendship with Rumi, however, aroused tremendous jealousy, and one night Shams was murdered and thrown down a well.

What is the purpose of spiritual efforts?

The Lion Tattoo

This story also involves a lion and a human being, though as we shall see, in a totally different manner. Now, it was the custom of the people of Qazvin to tattoo themselves on their bodies, hands and shoulders, as they believed that this would prevent evil and harm from befalling them. And so it happened that one day a man of that city went to the barber (for in those days it was the barber who tattooed people), and asked him to tattoo his shoulder blade.

'What figure do you want me to tattoo, my brave?' enquired the barber.

'Tattoo the figure of a raging, ferocious lion. The more raging and ferocious the better!' declared the man, 'you see, I was born under the sign of Leo, and only a ferocious lion could ever satisfy anyone born under this sign.'

So the barber asked the man to be seated and to remove his shirt, while he busied himself preparing the needle with which he would draw the tattoo. No sooner, however, had he gently placed the needle on the man's shoulder so as to measure exactly where to begin the design, did the man cry out in pain and alarm.

'Noble sir! You have slain me! I am in mortal pain! Let me ask you what are you drawing?'

The puzzled barber replied, 'Why, a lion, as you requested.'

'And may I ask with which part you were intending to begin?'

'With the tail. I normally start with the tail,' the barber replied.

'Then I beg you to omit the tail. A lion is not any less ferocious if he lacks a tail. Omit the tail, for the prick of the needle nearly made my heart fail.'

So the barber began to work again, but once again, no sooner had he placed the needle against the man's skin did he yell out in anguish.

'Which part of the body are you now drawing?' he yelled.

'This is the ear,' replied the barber.

'Then let him be without ears! A lion does not need to hear to kill his prey. I beg of you omit his ears!'

And so the barber once again began to work, and once again the man yelled out in pain.

'Which part of the body now, dear sir?'

'This is the belly of the lion.'

'Let him lack a belly then! The picture is full enough already. What need for a belly?'

At this point the barber flung down the needle in anger,

'Whoever saw a lion without a tail, ears or a belly? My dear sir, you came to me and asked for a ferocious, raging lion — the most ferocious in Qazvin, you impressed upon me. But no sooner had I delicately placed the tip of the needle against your shoulder blade did you cry out in alarm. First no tail, then no ears, and now no belly! You ask for the qualities of a lion but are afraid to go through any pain that may impress these qualities upon you. Unless you patiently bear the pain of the trial, how can you ever expect to achieve anything?'

Whoever saw a lion without a tail,
ears or a belly?

The Camel, the Ox and the Ram

One day a camel, an ox and a ram were ambling along chatting to each other, when they stumbled across a tuft of barley grass. Now, as it happened, all three were hungry, and there is nothing like a tuft of grass when you are feeling hungry (if you are a camel, an ox or a ram, that is).

There was only one problem, as the ram explained, 'If we divide this tuft into three, then none of us will be satisfied. There must be another way.'

'You are right,' replied the ox. 'I have a suggestion. Let the one amongst us who is spiritually the most senior have it all. I think that is the fairest decision.'

'Excellent idea,' declared the ram. 'A most excellent idea. And since I was once pastured with that ram that Abraham sacrificed instead of Isaac, the tuft of grass should rightfully be mine.' With these words the ram advanced towards the grass, feeling well pleased that the matter had been so successfully concluded.

'Wait a minute!' cried the ox. 'I have something to say. You may have been with the ram that Abraham sacrificed instead of his son, but I was yoked in the team that Adam ploughed with when he left Eden. Surely that makes me the most senior spiritually, and therefore the grass should be mine! So please, I beg you, out of my way!'

'I don't recall any oxen in the story of Adam.' The ram by now was getting rather cross. 'Fruit, yes — but an ox? I don't think so. What I do know for certain is that I was present when Abraham sacrificed my cousin.'

'Yes!' retorted the ox stubbornly, and with some anger. 'Your cousin, because you were probably hiding. Now out of my way! Let me eat this grass so that we can be on our way.'

'NEVER! You have insulted me sir, and I demand an apology!'

The situation was getting serious by now, with the ram and the ox squaring up to each other. In the meantime the camel, who had been watching all this unfold in the languid manner that only camels possess, took a couple of steps forward, strolled past the ox and the ram who were arguing furiously about their spiritual purity, and plucked hold of the grass. Holding it above their heads so that neither could reach it, he now began slowly to chew on it.

'You know,' he told his two travelling companions, 'I am not very bright and know little about genealogy or chronology, but I know that I am taller than the two of you, and that must have some spiritual significance.'
In the same way, human beings' upright nature is spiritually significant as it carries with it the responsibility to be morally upright.

One day, Rumi was seated with his disciples in a circle next to the bank of a pond. While he was discoursing on a point the frogs in the pond started to croak together to such an extent that his voice could barely be heard. Then, in a loud voice, Rumi shouted to the frogs, 'What is this noise? Do you want to give this discourse or should I give it?' Immediately the frogs ceased croaking and said no more. When Rumi had finished his talk, he went to the pond and cried out, 'Now you can talk.' And the frogs went back to their croaking.

In another story we are told that one day Rumi asked a young disciple to get him a large quantity of sweets. The disciple was astonished by this request, for Rumi had a reputation of eating only what was necessary to keep him healthy. 'So,' he thought to himself, 'all night he pretends to be praying, while instead he is eating to his heart's content.' Nevertheless, the disciple did as he was asked. Rumi took the plate, covered it with a napkin, and headed out to the outskirts of the city. The disciple secretly followed behind, eager to find out what was going to unfold. He was astounded when he saw Rumi stopping near an exhausted mother dog who had just given birth to six puppies and was lying in some ruins too weak to feed herself.

Rumi then leant down and began to feed her by hand. When the disciple saw this he was overcome with shame at his earlier thoughts, and rushed to help Rumi feed the dog. 'It has been a week,' Rumi told him, 'since this poor dog has eaten anything. She cannot leave because of her small ones.' But when the disciple asked Rumi how he had known about the plight of the dog, he simply replied, 'God has transmitted her complaints to me and ordered me to console her.'

In yet another story Rumi was preaching to some citizens of Konya who had assembled in the market place. As the sun began to set people wandered away until only a pack of dogs who had formed a circle around him kept him company. Rumi continued discoursing, and when a passer-by pointed out that he was talking to dogs Rumi replied, 'Do you not see how they are wagging their tales and growling happily? I swear by God the Almighty that these dogs understand our spiritual wisdom.'

Rumi uses the imagery of a dog wagging its tail to illustrate another important point in his teaching. He writes that if a poor man hears that in such and such a city there lived a wealthy and generous man whose habit it was to bestow gifts and favours, he will naturally go there in the hope of sharing in

that wealthy patron's bounty. If that is the case, then if God's bounty is as renowned as it is, then why do we not beg of Him and hope to receive a gift or a favour?

We sit in indolence, Rumi tells us, saying, 'If God wills, then He will give it to me,' but we don't ask Him or plead with Him or beg Him. A dog, that has no reason or logic, when it is hungry and has no bread to eat comes up to us and wags its tail, as if to say, 'Give me bread. I have no bread, and you have bread.' 'Wag your tails,' urges Rumi, 'and desire and beg of God; for in the presence of such a Giver, to beg is required. If you have no fortune, ask for good fortune from the One who possesses great wealth.'

But of course, given his origins, Rumi's favourite animal was the camel; and his poetry and discourses are full of references to this animal, which is also mentioned in the Qur'an. In one story a Caliph is awoken from his sleep by some infernal noise on the roof of the palace. When he looks out of his window to see what is happening he spots a group of men busy searching for something.

'Who are you?' he bellowed, 'and what are you doing on the roof of my palace?'

'Please excuse the noise,' replied one of the men, 'but we have lost our camel and are looking for it.'

The Caliph was astounded. 'Looking for a camel on top of a roof! Whoever heard of anything so ridiculous!'

'Not as ridiculous,' replied the man who, as often is the case in Rumi's stories, turns out to be a saint, 'as finding a wealthy Caliph who is also pious!'

The words struck home, and we are told the Caliph abandoned his wealth, donned the woollen garment of the Sufis and joined his companions in their search for the 'Camel of Love.'

Animals also played a large part in saving Konya itself from the Mongol threat that had forced Rumi's family to flee from Balkh. 'I am the punishment of God.' These chilling words, uttered at the turn of the 13th century, could only have been spoken by one man, a man whose name till today stands for destruction, death and despair. These were the words of Genghis Khan. For a period of forty years Mongol hordes from the steppes of Central Asia swept through the Muslim world, leaving a trail of terror and death. City after city was sacked and plundered and the inhabitants put to the sword. Not even Baghdad was spared, and in 1258, to the horror of the Muslims the Caliph himself was put to death as the Mongols rode their horses through the city's mosques. A couple of years later Damascus and Aleppo fell, and both suffered similar fates. In Konya Rumi's family had found an oasis of calm in a desert of destruction and terror, and for a few years the terrible threat posed by the Mongol armies was kept at bay. But no longer. Nothing it seemed could halt the destruction and devastation of every great Islamic city.

And yet, quite remarkably Konya survived, and though historians may well point to political and strategical reasons for its survival, the city's inhabitants were in no doubt. Rumi had saved Konya. The legend goes that when the Mongol army besieged the city of Konya everyone despaired, fearing that the terrible fate which had befallen other cities would now befall them. In their panic and anxiety the people rushed to Rumi pleading for his help. Rumi, perhaps more than anyone, was well aware of the danger which the city now faced, but he listened calmly to the frantic pleadings now made to him, and then reassured them that he would do what he could. Then he asked to be left alone for the rest of the night.

A few minutes before dawn, Rumi left his house alone and climbed a hill which was situated behind the city's public place. In view of the Mongol army he performed the dawn prayer. The Mongols were astonished and enraged by what they saw; a solitary man, dressed in blue with a grey turban, standing in perfect serenity and oblivious to their presence, praying. It was an act of defiance which they could not tolerate, and they tried to shoot arrows at this man, but despite their efforts their arrows simply fell at their feet. They then tried to mount their horses to climb the hill to kill him, but no horse would advance. In the meantime, the inhabitants of Konya were watching in awe all this unfold.

It was not long before news of the man on the hill reached the Mongol commander who, full of fury, was determined to have him killed. Sending his best cavalry, he ordered them to return with this man's head. But just as before, the horses stubbornly refused to climb the hill, throwing their riders off their backs. When this news reached the commander he flew into an even greater fury and stormed out himself on horseback, vowing to kill whoever was on top of this hill. But once again the horse threw him off. He then attempted to climb the hill on foot, but to his amazement he found that his feet were not obeying him and remained rooted to the ground. Now, the Mongols may have been ferocious and brutal, but they were not fools, and they recognised that they were coming against a force far greater than their own. It was only then that the commander admitted the greatness of the miracle which was taking place, and he now returned to his camp and ordered that the siege be lifted and the city of Konya be spared.

It is not at all surprising to learn that the horses of the Mongol cavalrymen stubbornly refused to climb the hill, for it seems that Rumi, like St. Francis of Assisi, another great saint who lived at the same time, had a special relationship with animals.

Look at every animal, Rumi writes, every animal, from the gnat to the elephant: all are members of God's family, and dependent on Him for their nourishment. What an excellent provider God is!

Chapter 6

One day, not long after Shams's disappearance, Rumi was walking through a goldsmiths' bazaar in Konya. Listening to the melodic hammering in one of the shops he began to turn in mystical rapture, asking the owner of the shop to join him. For a while both whirled in the bazaar. The owner then returned to his shop while Rumi continued to whirl for hours. The people of Konya were scandalised. They had thought that with Shams gone Rumi would resume his normal life; but now they were told that he was seen whirling in a bazaar with a goldsmith, a man so unlearned that he could not even recite the fatiha properly. But Rumi cared little, and when people complained that he had gathered bad people around him he replied,

'If those around me were good, I would become their disciple; but since they are bad, I take them as disciples.' Sultan Walad, his son, described him thus:

> *He never stopped listening to music and dancing;*
> *He rested neither in the day nor at night.*
> *He had been a scholar, he became a poet.*
> *He had been an ascetic, he became drunk with love.*

The Student and the Gardener

Next to the university in Baghdad there was an orchard, the trees in which were abundant with fruit. Though the entrance to the orchard was barred by a gate, and though a gardener kept a wary eye, its walls were low and its fruits tempting. So it was not surprising that students clambered over the wall and, much to the anger of the gardener, helped themselves to the delicious fruit.

One day a student entered the orchard and climbed the nearest tree and started to eat the fruits hanging from it. When the gardener spotted him he came rushing towards him.

'What are you doing?' he shouted. 'Get down from that tree! This is private

property! You cannot just walk in here and help yourself to the fruit. Come down! I tell you, come down!' But the student ignored him and continued to munch contentedly on the fruit.

'This is God's garden,' he told the gardener smugly, 'and I am eating from God's fruits, given by Him.' For you see, the student was studying philosophy, and he was now testing his knowledge on the gardener.

'You are right,' the gardener replied, nodding his head. 'Carry on eating.' The student was delighted by his argument — clearly his hours of studying had not gone to waste. He had outsmarted the simple gardener and now he could eat to his heart's content. So philosophy was useful after all. He looked forward to telling his friends, who would surely marvel at his brilliance and scholarship.

An hour later, having eaten his fill, the student climbed down from the tree, but no sooner had he reached the ground than the gardener rushed towards him with a stick and began to beat him with it around the head. 'What are you doing?' the student cried out in alarm, trying to fend off the blows raining on his head. 'What are you doing? You are hurting me!'

'This is God's stick,' replied the gardener (who clearly was also a student of philosophy), 'and I am beating you with God's stick, given by Him.'

We must be responsible for our actions, Rumi tells us. When a gardener tells

a student, 'Don't eat the fruit,' and the student eats it and the gardener hits him on the head with a stick, it is not right for the student to say, 'I ate the fruit and it hurt my head.'

The Sultan and Ayaz

Many years ago there lived a mighty Sultan who ruled over a powerful land. Being the Sultan, he had many enemies and few friends. Such is the price one has to pay for power. The age in which he lived was one full of threats and plots, and the Sultan's life had to be constantly guarded by the finest, strongest and bravest men of the land. Now, from among the Sultan's guards there was one Ayaz, who was by far the strongest and bravest. Such was his courage and his loyalty that all the Sultan's enemies were afraid of him. Wherever the Sultan went Ayaz was by his side, his eyes always alert for any possible threats, his hand constantly on his sword. Now, in those days the Sultan's guards were well rewarded in riches and gifts, and over the years Ayaz became fabulously wealthy. Soon, for such is also the nature of those who guard the Sultan, he too gathered enemies around him: guards and other courtiers who were jealous of the fact that he had become the

Sultan's favourite, and who were envious of the wealth that he had accumulated.

Now, Ayaz's enemies watched him closely, hoping to spot a sign of disloyalty or a hint of ambition which they could use to discredit him in front of the Sultan. But Ayaz remained faithful, strong and loyal, always by the side of the Sultan. Or almost always, for those planning his downfall noticed that every day at the same hour, Ayaz would discreetly leave the Sultan's side and would disappear into his chamber for a few minutes.

'Surely he must be plotting against the Sultan!' remarked one of Ayaz's enemies.

'Or hoarding his treasures in preparation for a coup against the Sultan,' gleefully noted another.

There is nothing easier in the Sultan's court than to spread a rumour, and it was not long before the court was abuzz with stories about Ayaz's daily disappearances and the sinister reasons behind them. Soon those rumours reached the ears of the Sultan himself.

'Think nothing of them!' he joked to his ministers, 'Ayaz is loyal. He has stood by my side for nearly twenty years.'

'But he is ambitious, my liege,' said the vizier.

'And wealthy,' pointed out a courtier.

'Ambition and wealth ... a very dangerous combination,' murmured a minister.

And so, despite his words the Sultan began to think, and he did not like what his brain told him. Maybe he had misjudged Ayaz. Perhaps he had given him too much wealth. It could be that he was plotting. He could take no chances. Ayaz had to be arrested!

But not all those who were in the Royal Court suspected Ayaz, and the Sultan's wife, who was an intelligent woman and who could see what the courtiers were brewing, now spoke to her husband.

'Ayaz has been nothing but loyal,' she told him. 'Do you not recall when he saved your life last year?'

'It was his job to do so,' retorted the Sultan sharply, for by now the rumours sweeping the court had become fixed in his mind as truths. 'In any case you do not understand the nature of power.'

'That may well be true, my husband,' the Sultan's wife replied patiently, 'but I do know what loyalty is. What about the time when you fought the Mongols? Where were the courtiers who are spreading these baseless rumours then?'

The Sultan remained silent as he recalled those terrible days when he went out with his army to fight the Mongols, and how after the first skirmish he had been cut off from his troops. Many of those around him fled in terror, while others were slaughtered by the Mongols. Soon the only thing that stood between the Sultan and certain death was Ayaz's sword.

'And for three days he protected you while you were wounded and in a feverish state.' The Sultan's wife knew her husband well, and knew what he was thinking. 'He carried you from one hiding place to the next, one step away from the Mongols who were desperate to capture you, until he brought you to safety. I may not understand politics, but I know that Ayaz is not disloyal.'

'But what about his daily disappearances? Where could he be going? What could he be plotting?'

'If you want to find out, it is simple. Send someone to follow him and spy on him. I have a loyal servant who is discreet. Let us first find out what Ayaz is doing before we condemn the poor man.'

And so the next day when Ayaz disappeared into his chamber, he was followed unawares by one of the of the Sultan's wife's servants. But what the servant saw was so astonishing that he rushed back to inform the Sultan.

'So, did you follow him?', the Sultan asked the servant, having cleared the

court so that the only other person there was his wife.

'I did, my liege.'

'And what did you see?'

'He entered into his chamber, my liege, but I managed to sneak a view from a window. He did nothing.'

'Nothing?' The Sultan was astonished.

'Well, almost nothing. All he did was look for a few minutes at a pair of old, worn-out shoes and a tattered coat: clothes that should have been thrown out years ago. That was all.'

The Sultan was completely perplexed. 'Worn-out shoes? Tattered coat? What could this mean? Summon Ayaz at once!' he commanded.

A few minutes later Ayaz was summoned into the Royal Chamber.

'Ayaz, there have been many rumours sweeping the court.' The Sultan's voice was stern.

'My liege, there have always been rumours.'

'But these rumours concern you, Ayaz.'

'My liege, I am your closest guard. Inevitably there would be rumours about me.'

'Ayaz, I have had you followed into your chamber. Your disappearance needed to be … needed to be investigated!' Clearly the Sultan was feeling uncomfortable, for thanks to his wife, he too knew that Ayaz was loyal. Now he was informing his most loyal servant that he had been placed under suspicion and followed. No matter, he had to get to the bottom of this!

To the Sultan's surprise, Ayaz showed neither astonishment nor anger. 'It is only natural to have had me followed, my liege. After all your safety is paramount.'

'Ayaz,' the Sultan sighed deeply. 'What is going on? What is it about the coat and the shoes.'

'My liege,' Ayaz replied, 'the old, worn-out shoes and the tattered coat were the clothes that I had on the day I first came to work here. They are a daily reminder of my poverty, and they are a reminder to be grateful for all the bounty that I have received from you. If I forget who I am, then I will forget to give thanks for your boundless greatness and kindness.'

In this way Rumi saw in Ayaz's attitude a model for the believer. By recognising his own poverty man gratefully acknowledges his Lord's bounty, and by accepting his limitations he recognises the unlimited grace of God.

There is another story about this Sultan: a short one, but long enough to show us why he was such a good Sultan. Now, apart from his wife whose advice was so important in the previous story, this Sultan had three other wives. It came to pass that one day, while he was in court, he was approached by his four wives, all at the same time.

'We have a request to make of you,' one of the wives spoke out. 'We wish to know which of us is the dearest to you.' The tone of her voice, and the fierce and determined look in the eyes of the other wives, left the Sultan in no doubt that this was a question to which an answer was required.

And so for a while he remained silent, his head bowed in deep reflection. Then, taking off a ring from one of his fingers, he spoke. 'Tomorrow this ring shall be in the apartment of the wife I love best. But for the sake of harmony, I ask you only this: may the one of you who receives this ring not boast or speak out, for I forbid jealousy and envy in my court. Let the one who receives the ring rejoice in silence, for she will know that she is my beloved.' The wives agreed to this and left the court satisfied, each one certain that the ring was destined for her.

The next day the Sultan ordered three rings to be made identical to the first, and placed one ring in each of his wives apartments.

On one occasion Rumi was asked by one of the students to explain wherein lay the spirit within the body. To this question Rumi responded by relating the most charming of stories. The following, about the cat and the meat, is one such story.

If this is the Cat, where is the Meat?

There once lived a man who was married to what may gently be called a difficult wife. The marriage was a loving one except for one thing: the wife constantly lied to her husband. It so happened that one day the husband invited a close friend of his to dinner. Since he was a dear friend, and since the husband wanted to honour him, he had bought from the butcher a fine piece of meat.

'Cook this meat,' he told his wife, 'for tonight we have company.' With these words the husband went off to work, his mind already on the feast that would await him in the evening.

A few hours later, while the sun was still high in the sky, the wife, who had all the intention in the world to cook the meat, began to feel hungry.

'What I will do,' she reasoned, with a logic of which she was proud, 'is to cook the meat and eat a tiny, tiny sliver. Enough to soothe my hunger, but so small that neither my husband nor his guest would notice.'

But what she had forgotten was that thoughts which occur while hungry have a logic of their own. Soon the meat was cooked and the aroma, a delicious mixture of spices and herbs, filled the room; and before long, as one mouthful followed another, as one 'oh, just another sliver' followed 'well, I will just finish that piece so it will look tidy,' the meat was all gone.

What a calamity! The wife had no money to buy another piece of meat. What would her husband say in front of their guest? There was only one solution, the wife reasoned. She would tell her husband that the cat had eaten the meat.

And that was what she did. 'Oh, my husband!' She ran towards him as he returned home that evening with tears in her eyes. 'The cat … the cat ate the meat!'

'The cat ate the meat!' the husband was clearly nonplussed.

'All of it,'she spluttered.

'All of it?'

'All of it.'

For a few seconds the husband remained silent. Then in a loud, menacing voice he called for his servant. 'Fetch me the cat .... and the scales!'

When the servant had done so, the husband weighed the cat and nodded to himself, lost in thought, his face perplexed.

'The cat ate all the meat?' he enquired once more.

'All of it.'

'Then it is a miracle!' the husband exclaimed loudly.

'What is, my dear husband?' asked his wife as innocently as anyone who has just eaten three pounds of meat.

'This morning I bought three pounds of meat.' The husband turned towards his wife, the cat in his hands. 'This cat weighs three pounds exactly. So tell me, my dear wife. If this is the cat, where is the meat? If this is the meat, where is the cat?'

So Rumi concluded, 'If you have a body, where is the spirit? If you are spirit, what is the body? That is not our problem to worry about. Both are both. Corn is corn-grain and cornstalk.'

If this is the cat, where is the meat?
If this is the meat, where is the cat?

Chapter 7

One day, we are told, in the year 1256, Rumi was walking with Husam ud-Din when he suggested that Rumi should compose a treatise in verse which contained his teachings.

'If you were to write a book like that of Sana'i or Attar it would become the companion of many troubadours. They would fill their hearts from your work and compose music to accompany it.'

Rumi smiled and replied that this had already been on his mind, and took a piece of paper from his turban on which were written the first eighteen verses. Thus began the writing of the Mathnawi. Those first few verses that Rumi had written down and stored in his turban became known as the Song of the Reed, in which he tells of the longing of the reed flute for the reed-bed from which it has been cut.

> *Listen to the reed flute telling you a story and*
> *Lamenting the separation:*
> *Since I was cut from the stalk,*
> *My song makes men and women weep.*

Husam ud-Din wept with joy when he heard these words, and implored Rumi to write volumes. To this request Rumi replied, 'Chelebi, if you consent to write for me, I will recite.' And this is how it all began.

On one occasion Rumi was asked why it was that God sent a man as His Prophet and not an angel. To this Rumi replied by narrating the following story.

The Baby on the Roof

One day a young mother was busy working in her kitchen when her infant son, unbeknown to her, crept out of the room and managed somehow to climb the stairs which led to the roof of the house. When the alarmed mother noticed her son's absence she dashed up the stairs in panic, only to see her son playing on the roof, dangerously close to the edge. However, when she approached to pick him up he thought she was playing and dashed closer to the edge of the roof, the fall from which would have meant a certain death. When, on the other hand, the mother in her fear shouted at the infant, he began to cry and refused to come closer. The situation was most grave.

Hearing the commotion the woman's neighbours gathered around the house, some on the roof with the distraught mother, others beneath the edge of the roof hoping that they may be able to catch the baby were he to fall.

Oblivious to the danger in which he was, the baby continued to play. Upon this perilous scene came Imam Ali (ؑ), and naturally the mother rushed to him in her anxiety.

'My baby son is on the roof,' she explained frantically, 'if I approach him he thinks that I am playing and runs away from me. He will surely fall to his death!'

To these desperate words, Imam Ali (ؑ) listened carefully, but when he told the mother what she should do, her face blanched in horror. Surely the Imam must be in error!

'I believe you have another son a year older. What you must do is send him up on the roof as well.'

'But he too will fall to his death!' the distraught woman protested.

'You have no time to waste, woman!' Imam Ali (ؑ) replied. 'Your baby will fall to his death if you do not act quickly. If you wish to save his life, you must send your other son up onto the roof.'

What could the poor woman do? She now dashed home, picked up her other son, and tore up the stairs to the roof where she gently, and with great reluctance, left him. But the Imam was not being reckless: his reputation for wisdom was merited. For no sooner did the baby, still amusing himself

on the edge, see his brother, then he recognised him and crawled towards him and safety in order to play.

In this way Rumi explained that man, unaware of his plight, is playing dangerously close to the edge of damnation and Hell-fire. In His Love for him, God sends a messenger; not as an angel, but a man, easy to recognise and to identify with, whose life, full of opportunities and challenges, would offer us all solace and comfort. A man who could lead us from the edge to the centre.

Imam Ali (ع) and the Infidel

Though the earlier story demonstrated how wise and sage Imam Ali (ع) was, he was also renowned for his courage and bravery. Now, in the early days of Islam at times of battle when the two opposing armies faced each other, it was the custom for each commander to send forth two or three of his bravest fighters to challenge an opponent in hand to hand combat. It was, of course, a fight to the death, and both armies would watch these deadly duels urging their warriors on, for triumph in those duels was a good omen for the ensuing battle.

Given his courage and skill as a fighter, Imam Ali (ع) was always chosen by the Prophet to either issue or accept one of the challenges. And so it came to pass that battle after battle the Imam would advance sword in hand and confront one of the infidels. The conflict would be short, and would end with his enemy slain with the Muslim army's echoes of 'Allahu Akbar' resounding in his ears.

Now, this story revolves around one particular battle. The infidel who stepped forth to fight Imam Ali (ؑ) was a fearsome sight to behold, but that was no reason for concern, for the Imam had slain savage-looking warriors before. Slowly the two men circled each other gripping their swords, their eyes locked. In those duels it was crucial to make the first move and to strike first, but it could be fatal if that strike failed to hit its target, for then the attacker would find himself off balance and at his opponent's mercy. Any experienced warrior knew that; and on that particularly hot day both men preferred caution to haste, for a cautious warrior tended to have a longer life.

So if it took patience to slay your enemy, then patience it had to be, and Imam Ali (ؑ) simply chose to fend off the other man's thrusts and make no move forward himself. He had fought many, many duels, and as he looked into his opponent's eyes he could see the frustration and anger mounting. Occasionally the man would taunt him and challenge him to make a strike, but the Imam ignored him completely, his sole focus on his sword and his opponent's movements.

And then it happened: just as the Imam had seen in so many conflicts before. Unable to control his rage and frustration, the fighter charged at Imam Ali (ؑ), his sword raised menacingly above his head and aimed at the

Imam's neck. The whole incident could not have taken more than a few seconds; but a few seconds is all it took for Imam Ali (ع) to wait until his opponent had committed himself, to swiftly side-step the charge, and then nudge his enemy off-balance, so that by the time the dust had settled the man was on his back, his sword misplaced, and Imam Ali (ع) was looming above him.

He now raised his sword to strike the man, but just as he was about to deal the fatal blow, the man suddenly spat into the Imam's face.

'If you are going to kill me,' he snarled, 'then do so, for I will never accept this religion for which you fight.'

It was a terrible insult to spit in someone's face, and though the man was on the door-step of death, it seemed certain that he would now be slain in a more ferocious way.

Or so at least did the soldiers think, entranced as they were by the duel. But the fatal blow never came: and rather than strike the man, Imam Ali (ع) froze for a few seconds, and then, to the astonishment of everyone, slowly brought the sword down to his side.

'So slay me!' the man taunted. 'Why do you hesitate? Are you not man enough to kill?'

'I was going to slay you,' Imam Ali (ﺥ) replied calmly, 'but when we started this duel I was fighting for Islam as Allah told us to do in His Holy Book.

'That was my only motive for fighting, for I abhor violence and killing for its own sake. I fight, not because I wish to, nor to see my enemy slain, as some do. I fight, and on occasion I kill, because that which is sacred has to be defended. Nothing would please me more than to welcome you as my brother in Islam, for I gain no joy or satisfaction in slaying you. I seek no praise or reward, save to know that I have done what Allah wills.'

'But when you spat in my face I felt insulted as a noble Arab and angry as a man. For a few seconds my honour had been tarnished and my pride challenged. For an instant I felt anger coursing through my veins and I wished to slay you for this insult.'

'But thank God I did not; for just as quickly, I realised that to do so would be to simply satisfy a burning rage in me that would certainly, as night follows day, return to taunt me on another day. I understood that anger and hate and fury can blind us, making us act in ways that can only lead to greater anger, hate and fury. To satisfy the fire that burns inside us, that can rage up at a mere spit so as to blind us from following the right course of action, would lead only to perdition.'

'And at that moment when you spat in my face, I understood what our noble

Prophet (ﷺ) meant when he told us that the greater jihad was not against our enemies, whom we need to fight with a detachment born out of faith, but against the ego which lives within us, and that can so blindly lead us into error simply to satisfy its desires. And all for a spit. No, I will not slay you.'

Tears now filled the man's eyes as he listened to the Imam's words.

'By the soul of my father, I have never heard words so true. If this is your faith, then I wish to devote my life to it. I have fought many battles, but now I understand that my greatest battle lies ahead.'

On one occasion Rumi was asked as to why the Qur'an appeared so complex and difficult to understand.

The Qur'an, Rumi explained, was like a beautiful bride whose face was hidden behind a veil. Now, if an impatient and hasty suitor approached this bride, she would refuse to remove her veil. If you try to unveil her, Rumi explained, she will not show herself to you. If you simply discuss the Qur'an you will discover nothing and no joy will come to you. That is because you have tried to pull off the veil and the Qur'an refuses itself to you; you have been impatient and instead of applying yourself carefully and diligently in order to discover Its marvels you have been hasty and clever in a superficial way, loving your own pride — The Qur'an is saying to you: 'I am not that which you love.' But if you approach the Qur'an, (as the bride), with patience, sincerity and humility, then the veil will be lifted and you will see marvels.

Rumi accepted many disciples and never discriminated between men and women. On the rare occasion, however, when he turned down the request of someone who wanted to join him, and if asked why he had acted so, he may have replied, 'Well you see, I don't have a sieve.'

The Goldsmith who Refused to Sell Gold

One day, in a village not far from Konya, a man came to a goldsmith.

'Give me the scales,' he said. 'I want to weigh some gold.'

'I am sorry,' replied the goldsmith. 'But I don't have a sieve.'

'A sieve? But I did not ask for a sieve. I asked for some scales to weigh my gold,' the man insisted, clearly taken aback by the goldsmith's answer.

'I am really sorry,' replied the goldsmith. 'But, you see, I also don't have a broom.'

'What are you saying?' exploded the man. 'Do you think I am a fool? A

sieve! A broom! I asked you for some scales to weigh my gold. It is not I, but you who are a fool. I will take my gold elsewhere.' And with these words the man stormed out.

Now, watching all this was the goldsmith's assistant, who was clearly also puzzled by what he had witnessed.

'I do not understand,' he ventured to the goldsmith. 'The man came in requesting the scales — a request which is certainly not uncommon — and you tell him that you do not have a sieve?'

'I also don't have a broom,' the goldsmith added. Then, noticing how perplexed his assistant seemed, he explained.

'I am not a fool. Very few goldsmiths are.' Did you notice the man as he walked in? He was trembling, and his hands constantly shook. Now, of course, he may have contracted an illness that would cause this, but given his age and his state, as well as his short temper, I would hazard a guess that a considerable amount of his time was spent in wine taverns. Now, did you notice the gold he was carrying? It consisted of the tiniest filings. So what do you think would happen if I gave him the scales? His hands shake so, he would drop the filings. Then he would say, 'O goldsmith, bring me a broom so that I may hunt for my filings among the dust.' And if I did agree to this request, he would end up gathering the dust and the gold, and then would say, 'O goldsmith, give me a sieve so that I can separate my gold

from your dust.' You see, it is simple. I saw the ending of this story from the beginning, and sent him on his way.

In this way Rumi as a spiritual master understood the state of the souls of his disciples and the direction in which these souls were heading, and separated those who were sincere in travelling the spiritual path from those insincere or incapable of doing so.

To those who were sincere and devoted, however, Rumi was generous in his time and teachings; and if on occasion their rashness or immaturity meant that they spoke out of turn, he would gently correct them.

I saw the ending of this story from the beginning.

Where is the Crescent Moon?

It was, we read in the Mathnawi, the eve of Ramadan, and all the people of a town had headed to the nearest hill trying to spot the crescent moon which would signal the start of the holy month. The evening was partly cloudy, so the men had to crane their necks and concentrate hard. Then suddenly one of them shouted in glee, 'There! There, I see it! I see the crescent!' The governor of the town came rushing to the man, for it was customary for him to announce the sighting of the new moon. But though he looked carefully into the section of the sky where the man was pointing, he could see nothing.

'Where?'

'There!'

And once again the governor stared into a crescent-less black sky.

'Where exactly?'

'There! There!' The man continued to point.

Clearly there was no crescent, but equally clearly the man, who was known for his truthfulness, was seeing one and pointing to it. Suddenly the governor turned to the man.

'Go wet your hand,' he ordered. And when the man had done so he told him to wipe his eyebrow.

'Now do you see a crescent?'

The man looked skyward into the black sky, and his face took on a puzzled look. 'It is most peculiar. I no longer see the crescent.'

The governor smiled. 'It was not the crescent you saw, but a hair from your eyebrow which had fallen across your vision.' But when he saw that the man had become crestfallen with sadness and embarrassment he patted him gently on the back.

'You are a lucky man, my friend. If you had not wiped your eyebrow, you would have seen the crescent every day.'

Rumi was extremely strict when it came to observing religious observances. Referring to prayer and fasting, he stressed, 'It is a duty to practise them, to perpetuate them, and to pledge to follow them.'

We are told that once, in the dead of winter, he spent a whole night in prayer in the mosque. As he prayed, he became overwhelmed with emotion and wept so much that his beard, wet from his tears, froze and clung to the ground. Indeed, most nights were spent on the terrace, even in the coldest winter (for the cold prevented sleep), praying until dawn. When Rumi came down from the terrace, his servant would help him take off his shoes and would weep as he saw his master's feet bleeding from the cold.

Both wealthy and poor came to study with Rumi, and though he welcomed the rich merchants who attended and often gave away trunks full of precious materials to charity, his sympathy clearly belonged to the poor. On one occasion, he was criticised by some of the elite of Konya for accepting anyone, whether they were a tailor, a weaver, or even a greengrocer. Whereupon Rumi reminded them of the origins of the famous sufi leaders to whom they were so devoted; Abu Bakr an-Nassaj (the weaver), Junayd al-Qawariri (the glass-blower), Haddad (the blacksmith) and al-Hallaj (the cotton carder). He would always try to help the poor, and wrote many letters pleading for help for them. Could so and so not be exempt from taxes? Could he not be given a job? Could she not be granted some money to pay off her debts? And so on. At the same time, Rumi never

tolerated any vulgar or crude behaviour from his disciples. His nature was refined in the extreme, and he fully expected his followers to follow suit and to behave at all times with dignity and decorum.

You are a lucky man, my friend. If you had not wiped your eyebrow, you would have seen the crescent every day.

The Man who Dreamt of Cairo

In the Mathnawi Rumi relates the story of a man living in Baghdad who had wasted all his inheritance and had become poverty-stricken. Now, this man was pious and he prayed fervently to God to help him, and one night he heard in a dream a voice telling him that a treasure was awaiting him in Cairo. He travelled there, but since he had no money he was forced to beg. As he was wandering the streets he was picked up by the police who, thinking he was a thief, beat him up. However, when he told them about his dream, he spoke with such sincerity that he was brought to the Chief of Police who listened avidly.

'I believe you,' he said, 'but tell me, who would be so stupid to have made such a journey on the basis of a dream? I myself have dreamt that a treasure was awaiting for me in Baghdad at such and such a street. Yet I

have never undertaken that journey.'

To the man's amazement the Chief of Police mentioned the very house where he, the man from Baghdad, lived. He now understood that the cause of his misfortune was his own error. He returned to Baghdad where he found the treasure hidden in his own house.

This story holds a deep meaning. The conclusion is clear: the treasure that we are all seeking lies within us, but in this story Rumi wanted to emphasise another point, and that is that before the treasure can be discovered a journey is necessary. This journey is a spiritual one. For some in Konya and elsewhere, however, the dedication and sacrifices required meant their fleeing from the spiritual life, none more so than the court jester Dalqak.

Dalqak's Message

The King of Tirmid, we are told, had urgent business in Samarkand, and he needed a courier to go there and return in five days. Such was the urgency of the trip, that he offered many rewards to anyone who would make the journey — horses, servants, gold, and the robes of honour. Dalqak, the court jester, was out of town when he heard of this. Quickly he mounted a horse and rode at great speed to the King. He rode furiously, and two horses dropped dead from exhaustion under his whip. Finally, in the dead of night, he arrived covered in dust. Such was the noise that he made, and so distraught was his appearance, that panic swept the city. What possible calamity could have befallen that Dalqak the jester should be so overcome? Clearly an evil omen had occurred. Even the King, who had been awoken from his sleep by all the furore, became anxious.

'What is it, Dalqak?' he enquired.

But Dalqak was clearly out of breath and incapable of speaking, and he simply made a gesture as though to say that he needed more time. And so the King waited, and the court waited. All were anxious, for no one had ever seen Dalqak like this.

Usually he was a constant stream of jokes. Normally the King would be laughing so hard that he would fall to the floor. This was most peculiar and alarming. Everyone feared the worst.

Finally, when Dalqak had gathered his breath, he addressed the King. 'I was far from the court when I heard that you needed a courier, someone who could go to Samarkand and back in five days.'

'That is true,' the King replied.

'Well, I hurried to tell you,' exclaimed Dalqak, 'that I will not be able to do it!'

'What?' The King was totally baffled.

But Dalqak insisted, 'I don't have the stamina or the ability to do it. Don't expect me to be the one.'

Such is the nature of those who spend their lives in breathless pursuit of wealth, goods and happiness, instead of dedicating it to what is essential.

When asked once by one of his disciples whether there was a quicker way to God than prayer, Rumi answered, 'More prayer,' explaining that prayer should not simply be confined to the five daily ritual prayers, but should be constantly on the lips and in the heart of the disciple. For Rumi everything was prayer, and prayer was everything. He once described himself as completely transformed into prayer, 'so that everyone who sees me wants a prayer from me.' He was well aware of the power of prayer, and often criticised those who called upon God only in time of danger and then forgot Him afterwards.

And yet, even if one has forgotten God for a long time, Rumi always stressed that it was never too late to turn to Him in repentance. To illustrate this, he related the story of the old musician whose voice had become 'like the voice of an ass.'

Is there a quicker way to God than prayer?
More prayer, Rumi answered.

The Old Musician

There once lived a musician who as a young man was blessed with a remarkable voice. People from all lands flocked to listen to him, and it was not long before caliphs and sultans too requested to listen to this prodigious talent. Wealth poured in, as did fame, and so attracted was the young man to both that he continued to sing every night and most days as well.

The years passed and the man's fame began to dwindle. His voice, so strong and clear when he was young, began to break up; and though he gargled with many potions it was clear to everyone that his best days were behind him. In any case there were many other young, talented singers to sing to caliphs and sultans, and it was not long before the man had been completely forgotten, to such an extent that whenever his name was mentioned, people would simply look blank.

Now at the age of seventy, the man was all alone. His wealth, once enormous, had disappeared a long time ago, and his friends had left at about the same time. As for his voice, all that was left was a croaking hoarseness that was extremely painful to listen to, except that there was never anyone around to listen to it. Death was not long off now, and as the man reflected on his life he became aware that he had not once thought about God. He had been so busy singing, gathering wealth, romancing women, that looking back he could not recall a single prayer that he had ever made in gratitude for the remarkable talent he had been given. He did not even know how to pray. Though he had often walked past mosques and caught glimpses of men bowing down, he had paid little attention. Now it was too late, he had ignored God all his life and God, he believed, would choose to ignore him.

But even if God might not listen, the old man felt overwhelmed with the desire to give thanks. And so he bowed down for the first time in his life; and since he did not know how to perform the ritual prayer, he simply spoke:

'You gave me ample life,
And gave me ample time,

You were so kind to one
Who is so lowly, O God!

For seventy years I was rebellious here,
But You did not withhold Your bounty for one day!

'Today I cannot earn;
I am old, I am Your guest.

I'll play the harp for You,
For I belong to You.'

The old man then began to play the harp and sing in a voice which once made people sigh in awe, but which now simply screeched. And this time the man sang not to Caliphs or Sultans, nor did he sing for money or beautiful ladies. This time he sang to God. He could offer nothing else to Him but a talent which was long exhausted.

And, Rumi assures the reader, God accepted the old man's prayer, for God hears and answers the prayer of each and every one, though it may not be uttered in a manner approved of by theologians. 'Call me and I shall answer you,' we are told in the Qur'an (40/62), and though some have interpreted this verse symbolically, Rumi assures us not only of its literal truth, but urges us to call on God in any language.

The Sindhis like the expression of Sind,
The Hindis like the expression of Hind.

Once there lived a man who spent years praying to God without hearing any answer. In a moment of weakness Satan spoke to him, whispering in his ear that since there had been no answer, his prayers had gone to waste and he should cease. But then the man heard the Divine Voice:

> *Your call 'O God' is My call 'I am here.'*
> *Your supplication is My message dear,*
> *And all your striving to come closer to Me*
> *Is but a sign that I draw you to Me.*
> *Your loving quest and pain*
> *Signs of My grace!*
> *In each 'O God'*
> *A hundred 'Here's My Face.'*

I'll play the harp for You,
For I belong to You.

Rumi knew when he began dictating the sixth book of the Mathnavi that this would be the last part of the great work. After pouring out more than 55,000 verses of poetry he was exhausted. In addition, he devoted his days to his disciples and his nights to prayer. He used to say, 'If we allow ourselves to rest, who will bring a cure to those unfortunate sleepers? I have taken charge of them all and have asked God to give them to me. If He so wishes, I can lead them to perfection, free them from the consequences of chastisement and help them climb the ascending degrees of Heaven.' When he fell ill, Rumi knew that death was near, and when friends and disciples came to call upon him, he consoled them, reciting poems about the meeting with God. When Konya was suddenly struck with several earthquakes, the

disciples feared the worst, and on the night of 17th December 1273, at the age of sixty-six, in the city of Konya, Rumi passed away.

The funeral itself was a remarkable event. Men, women and children followed the corpse to its burial site. Everyone was crying, and most of the men were wailing aloud and tearing their clothes in grief. The members of all communities were present: Christian, Jew, Greek, Arab and Turk, all recalling how Rumi's humility, love and tolerance never differentiated between religions. His words now echoed in their ears: 'There are many ways to search, but the object of the search is always the same. Don't you see that the roads to Mecca are all different, one coming from Byzantium, the other from Syria, others running through land or sea? The roads are diverse, the goal one ... When the people arrive there, all quarrels, disputes or differences that occurred on the road are resolved. Those who were saying to each other on the road, 'you are wrong,' or 'you are an infidel,' forget their differences when they arrive, because there the hearts are in unison.'

A man gives one coin to be spent among four people.

> *The Persian says, 'I want angur.'*
> *The Arab says, 'Inab, you rascal.'*
> *The Turk says, 'Uzun!'*
> *The Greek says, 'Shut up all of you. We will have istafil.'*

They begin pushing each other about, then hitting each other with their fists — no stopping it! If a master of many languages had been there he could have made peace and told them:

> I can give each of you what you want
> With this one coin. Trust me, keep quiet,
> And you four enemies will agree.

> I know a silent, inner meaning
> That makes of your four words one wine.

For what they all wanted was 'grapes,' but they each used different words.

Although Rumi wanted to be buried simply, his wealthy admirers built a magnificent dome over his tomb, known as the Green Dome. To this dome millions travel from all over the world in order to visit the tomb of Mawlana Jalal ud-Din Rumi.

Some come to pray and give gratitude, others come in search of solace and comfort. No matter, all leave soothed, for the loving presence of Rumi is as strong today as it was on the day he departed from this world to the next. And as they prepare to leave, in their souls echo Mawlana's words,

If you are seeking, seek us with joy,
for we live in the kingdom of joy.